THE GOOD HAND
OF OUR GOD

The Good Hand of Our GOD

Ruth Hitchcock

David C. Cook Publishing Co.
ELGIN, ILLINOIS—WESTON, ONTARIO

Foreword

In the seventeen years that I have known Miss Hitchcock, she has been a constant source of inspiration to me as well as to many other Chinese Christians both in mainland China and in Hong Kong. She is held by all who know her as one of those outstanding missionaries to China who have endeared themselves to the people whom they serve by their selfless ministry and deep love.

I can never forget the times she spoke in chapel services at the Alliance Bible Seminary in Hong Kong when I listened spellbound to her personal experiences in South China. I have also had the pleasure of reading her former booklet—a vivid account of the joy and heartbreak of her long years of service in China which is at once fascinating and edifying.

Early in 1974, during a visit to the States, I made a detour to Santa Barbara in order to enjoy fellowship with this saint of God, then in her eighties. I discovered that she was still engaged in various types of service—teen evangelism, preaching, writing and intercession. A soldier of the cross never retires.

I count it a great privilege to be one of her many friends and colleagues in the service of God. I pray that this book will be a great blessing to all who read it.

Hong Kong

PHILIP TENG
President, Christian and Missionary
Alliance Church Union
Hong Kong Limited

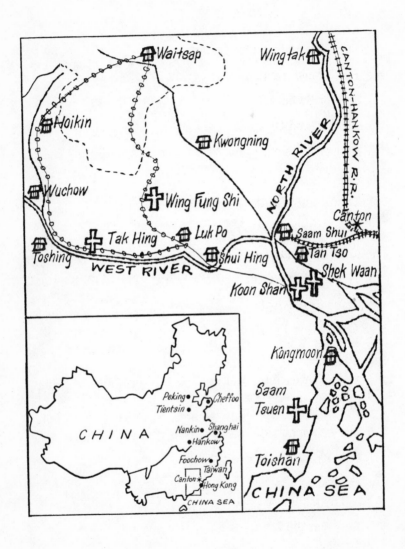

Contents

Preface

"I will sing of the mercies of the Lord for ever: with my mouth will I make known thy faithfulness to all generations."

My heart soars with the psalmist, but I don't have a singing voice. So instead I have attempted to write of God's mercies as I have experienced them, to make known His faithfulness at least to my generation.

I want to extend my thanks to friends and relatives who encouraged me to write this story; to Peggy-Jo Carlson who read the rough draft of the manuscript and offered many worthwhile suggestions; to my nephew's daughter, Nancy Potier, who did the typing; and most of all to my loving Heavenly Father who permitted me to experience so much of His tender care. Now He has given me time at the age of 80 to share the account of His goodness with others.

Santa Barbara, California   RUTH HITCHCOCK

A man fell into a dark, dirty, slimy pit. And he tried to climb out of the pit and he couldn't.

Confucius came along. He saw the man in the pit and said, "Poor fellow, if he'd listened to me, he never would have got there," and went on.

Buddha came along. And he saw the man in the pit and he said, "Poor fellow, if he'll come up here, I'll help him." And he too went on.

Then Jesus Christ came. And he said, "Poor fellow!" and jumped down into the pit and lifted him out.

from A FOREIGN DEVIL IN CHINA by John Pollock
© 1971 by World Wide Publications
Used by permission.

CHAPTER ONE

The Vision of an Empty Cart

*   *   *

O ne day a young woman who appeared to be mentally defective was brought to our lace school at Koon Shan by a Bible woman* from an outstation. She told us that a colporteur, selling Gospel portions, had found the retarded woman sitting at the door of a house and had offered her a Gospel of John. As he did so an older woman came out of the house and told him it was useless to offer her a book; she was crazy and didn't know anything at all.

"Crazy, is she?" asked the colporteur. "That's all the more reason why she ought to know about Jesus. Jesus can heal her."

The older woman was interested and wanted to know more about this person called Jesus. So the colporteur said he would send the Bible woman to come and see them. When she came, she was persuaded to take the poor demented woman to her own house to give the Lord a chance to show what He was able to do. But she soon found that caring for this one woman took too much time from her regular work. "The missionary lace school is the place for her!"

I wasn't too enthusiastic about taking her in, but the Christian girls all chimed in, "Let her stay! We'll take care

*For unfamiliar terms and names see the Glossary.

of her! We'll teach her!" And they won the day. Over their work they kept telling her in simple short sentences that Jesus is God, that He forgives our sins, that He loves and saves us. They told her over and over again to repeat the words, "Ee lai Ye-So" (trust in Jesus). It was a long time before she finally spoke those words, but the girls never lost their patience.

She used to go with them to the weekly prayer meeting held on the ground floor of our house at the foot of the mountain. When someone would stand up to give a testimony or to ask for prayer, she would stand up, too. The girl sitting next to her would pull on her clothes, telling her to sit down.

After about two months, she stood up by herself one evening at the prayer meeting. The girl sitting beside her was trying to get her to sit down when she suddenly said, "No, I have something to say." Then, speaking normally, she said that she had been out of her mind and couldn't grasp what people said. "But now I have come here and heard about Jesus, and I know He loves me. He has saved and healed me." From that time on to the day of her death, some 50 years later, Kwai Ling lived a normal, useful life as nurse for the children in our orphanage.

The orphanage, the lace-making—even my becoming a missionary to China: you could say it was mostly my parents' doing. When I was a little girl they were always entertaining missionaries and I loved to hear their stories.

On one occasion the Rev. Horace Houlding from North China was our houseguest. He was to speak at the evening prayer meeting in a nearby church, and even though I was only ten, I was allowed to go to hear him. He related an incident I would never forget.

On the great plains near the Yellow River, the peasants sow their wheat at the beginning of winter and then wait for the snow to cover it. During those snowy winter

14

months they are shut up in their houses, busy with indoor things such as shoe-making, spinning, weaving, and sewing. One winter a man came two days' journey by cart to the Houldings' mission station. He asked for a missionary to go back with him to his village during this quiet winter time to tell the people the good news which they had heard was available from these foreigners. Later on, the farmers would be too busy in their fields to listen, but now they were free. The missionaries thought this a wonderful opportunity. Who could return with the messenger? To their dismay, everyone was busy with the work they already had at the mission station. No one could be freed to go. Though the man begged them to find someone, he finally had to return alone with his cart to that village where they wanted to hear the Gospel. At the beginning of the next winter he appeared again—and again the bleak decision was reached. No one could go. The cart crept slowly back across the miles.

I sat in that prayer meeting, oblivious to everything but that village in China. They had asked for the Gospel and received an empty cart.

"I would have gone," I thought. But I was only a little girl. What would I have told them? In my heart the resolve grew: "Lord, when I grow up, I'll go."

My childhood home in Santa Barbara, California was beautifully situated between the coast range and the sea. Father worked outdoors on our fruit ranch, three miles out of town. His health had forced him to leave the management of our dry-goods store to my mother.

I graduated from high school in 1910 and went to Stanford University a year later, planning to major in German. I enjoyed languages and also studied Spanish and Italian. (Someday, I envisioned, our store would have a sign in the window: German . . . Spanish . . . Italian spoken here.) I was an avid tennis fan and spent my afternoons on the court. During the summer I usually worked in our store, and I loved this. Gradually the dream of becoming a successful businesswoman began to dim my missionary vision.

In my second year at college Mother suggested that two years at Stanford might be enough. "Travel is a good educator," she wrote. "What about taking a trip to China?"

With the word "China" the picture of that empty cart with the disappointed village at the end of the road burst back with such vividness that it shook me. I fled out into the woods where I knew I would be alone with God.

"Lord, I know I promised that when I grew up I'd go," I agonized. "But now I don't want to."

Tears flooded the confession from me over and over that afternoon. At last weariness pushed me to a decision: the only way to be fair and honest with God would be to take the trip to China and let Him have a chance to show me what I should do. I dreaded hearing Him say, "This is where I want you," but I had to expose myself to that possibility. Seldom has consent to a trip abroad been more grudgingly given.

In November another young woman from Santa Barbara was being sent to China as a missionary. Passage was booked for me on the same ship so that I could travel with someone I already knew. When we boarded in Seattle we found that the ship accommodated only 28 first-class passengers. Twenty-seven of them were Methodist lady missionaries and the twenty-eighth was a reluctant 20-year-old Stanford student.

It was 1913, and we were on a Japanese freighter in the North Pacific. When we steamed into a tossing storm the first day out from Puget Sound, I heard someone say: "I wonder if we've got a Jonah on board. With a storm like this . . ."

The words made me suddenly uncomfortable. Someone

running away from God? I didn't want to join the conversation. But the thought hovered until the weather finally calmed, several days later.

The evening before we were to arrive in Yokohama, I stood alone at the prow of the ship. The sun was setting. "I wonder if I'll ever do this again." The thought slipped into my mind. Hastily I turned my back to the beauty of the sun's gold path on the water.

"I'm going back to America to be a successful business-woman." Abruptly, to my surprise, the idea seemed less attractive. Another idea pushed hard against it: "Why not let God choose for you?"

That seemed reasonable, I had to admit. In relief I turned to the blue sky. "Lord, I'll do what You want me to. Just show me." I said it aloud, meaning it.

I had scarcely spoken the words when a flood of peace and joy came over me. It was impossible to describe, but that joy has been with me to this day.

CHAPTER TWO

The Transformation of a Tourist

*   *   *

When we arrived in Shanghai a few days before Christmas, I intended to head toward North China where the Houldings were working. But I learned that heavy snows would make such a trip impractical at least until February.

I had intended to go as quickly as possible to the end of the cart trail across the plains. Now, baffled, I remembered Miss May Jackson, a missionary from South China who had stayed with us the summer before. She had invited me to "return the visit" on the other side of the world. New friends in Shanghai knew her and gave me her address. I wrote her that I was coming and embarked for Hong Kong by a German liner.

I arrived in the British Crown Colony early in the new year, but no Miss Jackson met me. An English lady with whom I had become acquainted on the ship told me that St. George's House was a good place for a young woman traveling alone to stay. It was a pleasant hotel partway up the Peak.

When I got off the ship, I tried to use Shanghai coppers to pay the coolie who carried my suitcase, but he refused. "Not my kind money." He then almost dragged me to a money changer where I could change some of my Shanghai dollars into Hong Kong ten-cent pieces.

19

I got into a ricksha and said, "St. George's House." The coolie said something I didn't understand and took me a short distance to a row of sedan chairs. There I was told by means of gestures and many words (which included a few understandable ones such as "up," "St. George's House," and "Peak"), that to get to my hotel I must go the rest of the way by sedan chair.

When I arrived I found that the hotel was full. But the words had scarcely been spoken when an attendant came to the office saying that someone was leaving that morning. There was a room for me, after all.

From some missionaries to whom I carried letters of introduction, I learned that I had an incorrect address for Miss Jackson. Again I wrote to her, hoping she would come. In the meantime I was fairly bursting with enthusiasm at the new sights and sounds, enjoying glimpses of missionary work in Hong Kong. Happily I wondered what the Lord had in mind for me.

In due time Miss Jackson came. We went by train, third class, to Canton (about 80 miles from Hong Kong), where we spent a couple of nights with a Chinese Christian family and then set out for Shiu Hing where Miss Jackson had lived while studying the language.

The first part of the trip was 30 miles by train to a place where the West and North rivers converged. There the delta area began, extending south and east, and the railroad ended. We continued our journey westward for a few hours by a steam launch with deck accommodations only. It did serve food, however, and we each enjoyed a good plate of chicken and rice. On arrival at Shiu Hing, late in the afternoon, we went right to the home of Rev. and Mrs. Burtt, an elderly couple who received us cordially. They had a home for blind girls in part of the building they lived in and a preaching hall on one of the busy streets in the city.

The next day I was assigned to take a blind girl to church for the three Sunday services, morning, afternoon, and evening, each at least two hours long. I knew only one Chinese phrase, "shik faan," meaning to eat rice, which I had learned on the boat going up the West River. But there was little likelihood that the preacher would discourse on eating, so I sat in a blur of unfamiliar sound. In the middle of the third long sermon, the phrase "shik faan" leaped out at me. I all but jumped in my seat. I had understood something! Perhaps there was hope of my learning the language, impossible as it seemed.

On Monday we reached Koon Shan. A long, narrow market town, it lay between the river and a picturesque mountain that cropped up abruptly from the stretches of level land. The streets were narrow, paved with granite slabs, and lined with the gray brick walls of houses or the open doors of dimly lighted shops.

Near the end of the town we entered a dull, unattractive brick building. Inside were whitewashed walls; clean, tiled floor; and neat rows of desks. Smiling young women surrounded us with cordial greetings.

"Ping On," they chorused. "We wish you peace."

This was the schoolroom, a place where girls and young women learned to read, something unknown in that area until Miss Jackson had come with the Gospel about two years previously. Her dining room was a small room at the back from which a steep narrow stairway led to a tiny bedroom.

One bright-faced girl, who did the cooking and general housekeeping, soon had a hot meal on the table. As we ate, various Christians dropped in to greet us and ask if we were going to attend the meeting in the preaching hall at the other end of the town. It was all so simple and primitive, and the Christians so cordial! My heart was won to them that first night.

21

I spent two weeks or more with Miss Jackson, traveling with her to neighboring towns and villages by little covered rowboats or by the big, clumsy, passage boats towed by steam launch. Everywhere we went Miss Jackson kept sharing the Gospel, talking personally with individuals, or speaking to the large crowds that gathered to see these strange foreigners. As I accompanied her the conviction grew that this was the place where God wanted me to serve Him.

What I had feared and resisted that day in the woods near Stanford now delighted me. I told Miss Jackson I would return to work with her and she helped me make out a list of things to bring back with me. Later in Hong Kong I bought a Chinese New Testament and a Cantonese study guide. I was totally committed. To my mother I wrote:

I don't know whether it is good or bad news that I am about to tell you. But I feel as though I have to come back here to South China to work. I am afraid I could never be content to settle down quietly at home now that I have seen all these poor, hungry people and come to love them so much. To tell the truth, I wish I could settle down to work right away. It almost seems like a waste of time to go clear home when I might be accomplishing so much if I stayed. But then I am so unfitted for Bible teaching or anything of that sort. How I wish now that I had gone to Nyack [the only missionary-training college I knew of] long ago and learned things that would help me here. When I see the awful idol worship and then the hundreds of people who are eager to hear the Gospel, I just wish I could bring every true Christian from America out here and set them to work.

It seems awful for me to talk about coming back here when you need me so much at home. And that is the one thing that makes me sad. I dearly love the store and it is awfully hard not to think of going on with the work there. But this seems like so much bigger an opportunity to do something for God that it seems to have the stronger pull in my heart just now. When I first began to feel this way, I thought maybe it was just because it was all so new to me, but the more I see of the people, the more I love them and the more I want to do something for them. The dirt and smells and thieves don't seem to bother me a bit; I almost feel as though I were made for just such things. I study the language a little every day and with every new thing I learn, Miss Jackson looks at me in surprise. She says she does not know when she has seen anyone learn it so quickly. I am not telling this to praise myself, but it just looks to me like one more indication that I have found my little corner.

Dear Mother, pray that I may do just what is right, for I want to do God's will entirely. It would be dreadful to make a mistake in a thing like this.

I continued my original itinerary, and several months later Mother met my train in Santa Barbara. Without even a preliminary I said, "I'm going back to China to be a missionary."

"Praise the Lord!" Mother replied, although her blue eyes filled with tears. "When you were little, I told the Lord He could have you if He wanted you for His service."

CHAPTER THREE

Sink or Swim

* * *

I spent a few months at home preparing to go back to China. It didn't seem necessary to apply to a mission board to be sent out. I had seen the field and the need; the Lord had made clear where He wanted me. Miss Jackson was working there independently with her own means of support; and my folks felt that they could support me from the store income. My plan was to sail for China in September 1914, but World War I broke out in August and delayed my departure until December. I sailed from San Francisco and arrived in Hong Kong January 5, 1915, where Miss Jackson met me.

Ten days later we were on the big, clumsy riverboat between Canton and my new home. We were traveling in style for we had a "private room." I called it a "private cubbyhole"; it was a space about five by six feet wide and three feet high. We sat or lay on the matting-covered floor with all our hand luggage about us, since we couldn't stand up. A sliding board, serving both as door and window, opened onto the narrow deck. With the door closed, it was too dark to read. With it open, it was too cold to be comfortable. So we kept it closed except when the attendant came to refill our teapot with boiling water or bring us a tray of steaming hot food.

The front end of the boat was low and square, about ten

feet wide, rather than high and pointed as most Western ships are. Since it had no power of its own, it was towed by a steam launch.

Miss Jackson had rented a nice Chinese brick house for me in Sha Tau, just a few miles from Koon Shan. The husband of the teacher in the girls' school there was a well-educated man who spoke good Cantonese and was willing to be my language teacher.

I arrived on a cold wintry day. The one window in the living room of my new house faced northeast, the direction from which the piercing wind came. The window—of boards, not glass—had to be closed. Two small panes of glass in the tiled roof provided some light.

The following day I began my regular schedule: three hours a day with the language teacher, and attendance at Gospel meetings in the afternoon and evening. Miss Jackson had thought she would spend much of her time in Sha Tau, but as it happened, her work in other places increased so much that often she only stayed overnight every week or ten days. I was alone with the Chinese most of the time.

One evening during those first months a group of us were coming home from the evening meeting. A young man in the group asked me a question, which I understood. But I couldn't find the Chinese words with which to answer. I stumbled around, but had to give up.

Then the young man said, "Poor 'I Koo' [my Chinese name meaning "second sister" or "second aunt" and pronounced Yee Goo], she can understand to hear, but not understand to talk. Too bad!"

"Yes," I thought, "too bad, too bad! Can hear but can't talk. Will I ever learn?"

We arrived at our door. As soon as the street door and the inner door had been unlocked and opened, I hurried upstairs. My housekeeper's room was downstairs. I was very conscious of being alone. In all of China was there one other young girl who during her first few months of language study was left without another person who could speak or understand English for miles around? I began to pity myself: "Poor Ruth, why did you ever get yourself into such a place?" Suddenly the Lord spoke to me, "You didn't get yourself here. I brought you and I am with you. You are not alone." My heart melted. I knew He would enable me to learn the language.

Once when Miss Jackson was with me to interpret, I spoke in an evening meeting in the preaching hall at the far end of the town. A letter I wrote to my father describes it:

> I spoke for about 40 minutes on Matt. 11: 28, "Come unto me all ye that labor," etc., and that crowd of men, women, and children sat there drinking in every word. After the meeting a dear little girl, Ah Kwan, said she wanted to be a Christian and right then and there she prayed, asking God to forgive her sins.

The damp cold of winter changed gradually to the sticky warmth of spring and then by May to the humid heat of summer. I went to Koon Shan for a few days at Miss Jackson's request, and from there wrote home:

> I am having a few days without actual lessons, but the process of language absorption goes on just the same. I am also trying to memorize the book I am studying. The first of this month (June) I left off text books and am now reading almost anything in Cantonese I can get hold of. Just now I am reading "Tsan Tsau Ye-So" which might be translated "Draw near to Jesus." It is very well written and if I learn it by heart, it will help me in talking with the children; also with the women.

> Oh, by the way, I must tell you how very happy I was about two weeks ago when for the first time I talked with some women who had never heard of Jesus and

THE GOOD HAND OF OUR GOD

told them about the One True God and His love. You have no idea of the joy I had at finding I could really open my mouth and talk of the very thing I had come to China for. Since then I have had several opportunities on boats and have tried to make the most of each of them. The rainy Tuesday when I came here to Koon Shan, there were ten or more women in the women's room on the passage boat and all were eager to hear. When I first came, Miss Jackson said she thought I would be able to talk in six months and here at five months I am telling the story of Jesus to those who haven't heard. Oh! I am so happy! But I know it is not of myself; I give every bit of the glory to God. He wants me to do this work and so He is teaching and helping me.

By July it was raining almost continuously and the water was steadily rising. Three rivers were on the rampage. The delta outlets, in need of dredging, were too shallow to handle the water which had no place to go except over the dikes and across the countryside.

On July 16, 1915, I wrote:

This flood is worse than anything that has been known for over 300 years. The suffering is dreadful. I will try to be sane and logical and tell you all about it, if such a thing is possible with my head in such a whirl.

Sunday evening when I went up on the mountain just back of our house and looked down across the Koon Shan River, the country was like a vast lake with a few treetops and roofs sticking out of the water. Not a sign of all those acres of mulberry [silk was the major industry of our area]. We went to bed that night feeling it couldn't get worse, for it was already worse than last year.

At midnight I awoke and I shall never forget that night as long as I live. The last dike had broken and the water was pouring into our little neighboring village just across the river. It's so near we could hear

28

the people calling for help—men, women, and children shouting, crying and screaming for help, all in the blackness of the night.

And it was only a little while before word was brought us that the house where some of our schoolgirls sleep was likely to be flooded to the roof as there had been a very sudden rise in the whole river. We sent quickly and got the girls and their things out just in time. One of our Christians who is dreadfully poor had his house completely flooded, and he and his wife, aided by our helpers, moved their things to our house.

In the meantime, those awful cries continued, not only from the neighboring village, but also from the part of Koon Shan that lies nearest to the river, where people had already moved to the lofts of their little houses because of the high water. With this sudden rise they were caught between the water and the roof, with no possible way of escape, and they were drowned like rats in a trap.

The next day we were kept busy directing relief work and getting ready to leave for Hong Kong; and oh! the pitiful sights and heartrending tales of distress! Three people, who had absolutely nothing left to them but the few ragged clothes clinging to their bodies, came saying they were the only survivors out of their whole village. Another man was the only one left of his family. Others told of seeing people on the roofs calling for help with the water rising about them, but succor was impossible. One of our Christians, a fine businessman who had lost everything in last year's flood, was so in hopes of being able to pay off his debts this year. But the flood swept all away. He had thousands of silk worms which were just ready to be put on the frames for spinning their cocoons when the water filled his house to the roof and every worm was lost. He and his wife barely escaped with their lives.

At last that busy, weary day was over and we retired to rest with 30 people sleeping around us—men in the downstairs room and on the upstairs porch, girls in the dining room, and other people at our door and under the trees. The next morning we were up early so as to get off by the early passage boat for Canton.

We took a man with us to bring back rice for the destitute Christians if we could get any in Canton (all the rice shops in Koon Shan were flooded). Well, when we got to Canton, we couldn't land, the whole city was so flooded. Even Shameen, where all the foreign banks, offices, and consulates are located, was from five to seven feet under water—an absolutely unheard-of thing. There was nothing we could do but board the night boat for Hong Kong.

The Lord's hand was in this move. In Hong Kong Miss Jackson contacted a group of well-to-do men who were hurriedly forming a relief committee to do what they could to meet the terrific need. Almost within minutes she had the promise of 600 sacks of rice for distribution at Koon Shan, the first 100 sacks to be taken to Canton by U.S. gunboat that very night and then from there to be taken to Koon Shan by Standard Oil launches.

Thus our work for that summer was cut out for us. Located at the foot of the mountain we were in a strategic place to reach the refugees in their need. We gave a measure of rice (approximately 8 ounces) to each person three days a week. On alternate days the local Chinese Charitable Association distributed a bowl of thick rice porridge (congee) to all who applied. The number of daily recipients was frequently 5,000 during the first few weeks. Every day the Gospel was preached to the crowds, and as decisions were made, a Bible study class was started for the new believers.

It was high-pressured, on-the-job training for me. Every day I found myself a little more at home in the language. I mingled among the crowds, having personal talks. Sometimes I even led the Bible study class. The weather was hot and humid. I perspired profusely all the time, but I seemed to thrive in it. I learned to sleep on cool grass matting laid on boards and found it more satisfactory than a hot mattress.

As the months passed by, the water gradually receded and the people began returning to their water-soaked homes. Mosquitoes were everywhere and it seemed as though everyone was getting malaria, including me. Miss Jackson took me to Canton, hoping that better food would pull me out of it. But I got worse rather than better and probably would have died had Miss Jackson not called in Dr. Paul Todd to see me. His diagnosis was, "That girl needs quinine as badly as your starving Chinese need rice." I was taken to his hospital where he and his wife gave me tender, loving care and the bond of a life friendship was formed. I was released from the hospital just before Christmas and was so happy to be back in Koon Shan once more.

In the early spring I went to Shek Waan to live. For centuries it had been a center for pottery and it seemed as if everyone except the shopkeepers was engaged in making some form of pottery. I still had an hour of language study each day with a teacher, but most of my time was spent going out with the Bible woman to visit women in their homes and at work, to tell them about Jesus.

While I was there in 1916, a Mr. Poon, who had a rice shop, was led to the Lord. The testimony of his changed life was so striking that as the years went by he could claim that he had led 40 of his relatives from the Poon village (a mile from Shek Waan) to know the Lord.

In those days there was no airmail. By the time my parents learned of my severe illness, I was already out of the hospital and back at work. But they still said, "You need a change; come home for the summer." I protested that I was perfectly well again and was happy to stay. Mother replied that she wanted me to come and would meet me in Honolulu. That decided it; I would go.

Miss Jackson went to Hong Kong to see me off. On the way we talked about how good it would be if we could provide some sort of industrial work for girls and women, so that they could earn their own living and at the same time get some Christian education.

In our area thousands of girls and women worked from dawn to dark over steaming basins of water in the silk filatures, unreeling the fine silk filaments from the cocoons. There was no opportunity for learning to read, to say nothing of getting any Christian teaching. They had no leisure: no Sunday off or day of rest except at Chinese New Year, and that was only once a year. If we could organize an industrial department of some sort, they could earn their living working reasonable hours for six days. We could have a primary school for them at night and they would have all day Sunday for church services, other Christian activities, and rest.

As Miss Jackson said good-bye at the gangway of the ship, she added, "Now remember, if an opportunity for industrial work offers itself while you're home, be sure to take it."

CHAPTER FOUR

Of Lace and Orphans

*　*　*

Mother met my ship in Honolulu and we had a happy time going the rest of the way home together. Once there, it seemed natural to go with her to the store in the morning. I busied myself with something in the office until she called me to where she was talking to a traveling salesman, A. I. Potter, who had his samples spread out for her selection.

"Here's someone who wants to meet you," she said, "Mr. Potter is a Christian and is interested in missionary work."

We had a little conversation and then he asked, "Did you ever consider having industrial work for women and girls?"

"Why yes," I said. "What made you ask?"

Handmade lace was in great demand he said. In fact, the demand was greater than the supply. Why not have our women and girls make lace? He would be our salesman, without commission. He told of a place in Chefoo (North China) where lace was being made and suggested that on the way back I go there and find a teacher who would go with me to Koon Shan to teach lace-making.

Since this seemed to coincide perfectly with our sensed need, we concluded it must be the Lord's provision.

After two months at home, I again set sail. This time I left the ship in Shanghai and took a coastal steamer north to Chefoo, where Mrs. McMullen, a lovely big-hearted lady from the north of Ireland, had a school. The girls worked a half day making lace and studied the other half. I asked her if we could hire one of the older ones to go with me to Koon Shan to be a lace teacher. She discouraged me, saying that because of the differences in dialect, food, and culture, a northern girl would be very homesick in the South.

"What you want to do is learn to make lace yourself," she said. "Then you can teach it and won't have to bother with a teacher."

She assured me that it wasn't hard, and that I could very quickly learn all that was necessary. So I spent a week learning the intricacies of lace-making, an old art in Europe but new to me. When I left, I took samples of the equipment needed so we could have it made in Koon Shan.

The equipment was fairly simple; a board approximately 16 x 27 inches with a padded wheel was attached on one side for the "pillow" on which the pattern was worked. The padding on the wheel that I brought from Chefoo was coarse native felt, but South China had no such product. I used fine dried grass from our mountainside and covered it with a bit of outing flannel or other soft material. I had to send home to Santa Barbara for the brass pins used in shaping the pattern, but the Coats' sewing thread was available in Canton.

The bobbins on which the thread was wound had to be made on a lathe, but we found we could get them made to order quite inexpensively in Fat Shan, a city not far away. Some of the narrow lace patterns required 12 to 18 bobbins, but the wider ones needed 40 or more.

It took a while to get things started, but in March 1917, Miss Jackson wrote to my parents:

> What a great deal Ruth's trip home has meant to the work here! I wish you could look into our "lace

factory" and see the rows of happy faces over their work. There are 50 here now and about 15 coming in a few days. We are so happy. . . . The lace work is becoming the means of salvation to many. There have been some very bright conversations from the first.

Morning devotions were held every day for the girls and in the evenings they were taught to read and write the intricate Chinese characters. Some were already Christians when they came; some were just waiting to be shown the way; others weren't interested in anything but having a comfortable way to earn a living. The atmosphere of the whole place was joyful; the girls loved to sing over their work.

Many needy women found employment over the years in our mission industrial department, which later expanded to the weaving of cotton cloth, towels, mosquito netting, and silk quilts. More than a few who were demon-possessed came to know the Savior and experienced His power to deliver them from the forces of darkness.

We had learned that many girls lived right at the silk mills, coming a long distance from their homes for employment. Late at night they would sometimes play occult games and dabble in spiritism. One game in particular, which they called "Taking a trip through hell," left some of them demon-crazed, unable to continue their work, though others were left unscathed.

In the spring of 1918 Miss Jackson's health failed. She had been working beyond her strength for some time and it was inevitable that she would break down physically. I took her to the Todds' hospital in Canton where they gave her the best of care, but even so her recovery was slow.

Later in the same year, we received word that the United States government had placed an embargo on imported luxuries, including laces. Without a foreign market, our lace-making would have to be greatly curtailed, if not shut down. Eventually we found that small amounts of lace were allowed to pass the Customs, so a few old women who had no other means of support were allowed to continue their work. The girls and younger women had to find other employment. Yet many of them had found new life in Christ Jesus and had learned to read the Bible, so things were different for them.

My parents had been writing me to come home for a brief rest and I had been trying to persuade Miss Jackson to go for a much needed furlough. In November, just after the World War I Armistice, we left Hong Kong by a big Dutch ship, arriving in San Francisco just when the "flu" epidemic was at its height. Miss Jackson was met at the pier by her father and my nursing responsibilities were over. She never regained full health and did not return to China. She died about three years later.

In March 1919, refreshed by two months at home, I returned to the field, eager to go on with the work where Miss Jackson had left off.

One day a preacher from one of our outstations came to me with a request. His twin brother had been shot by robbers while he was guarding a boat loaded with coal for the silk mills. He left a young wife and baby boy. The young mother wanted to get rid of the child so that she could be free to marry again, and had even suggested giving him to the boat people. But the preacher said with great feeling, "This is the only son of my twin brother. I want him to have a Christian upbringing but I cannot take him myself. My wife is ill with tuberculosis and I have two small children of my own. Will you help me find some Christian home or institution where he may be placed?"

The request seemed reasonable. We made inquiries, but no place was found for a boy. It was maintained that no orphanage was needed for boys; the Chinese would always take care of male children themselves. I had been looking to the Lord for His guidance and it seemed that He wanted me to take the child whom we named Po Tak. I didn't want him to be one isolated child raised by a foreigner, so I asked the Lord that if it were His will, He would bring us others of His choice and provide for them. He did so and, strange to say, there have always been more boys than girls.

Kwai Ling, the woman who had come to the lace school two years previously with very low mentality, had been left to take care of my house while I was on furlough. When I came back, she continued to do the cooking and housework. And then when this six-month-old boy came into the family, her motherly heart opened to him. She had found her niche and was happy. God had prepared His choice for the orphanage work. Frequently, in later years, when I was being asked to take in another child and was about to refuse on the grounds that Kwai Ling already had more than she could manage, she might hear about it. She would then come around by the back door and ask to see me for a few minutes.

"Don't turn the little one away," she would say. "If she grows up with us, she is sure to be a Christian."

"But you already have more work than you can do, Kwai Ling. I don't want you to kill yourself off for just one more child. You're too valuable."

"Don't worry about me," she would reply with her cheerful smile. "The Heavenly Father will help me." The child had a home.

During the last year of World War I, the rate of exchange began dropping. When I first went to China, $1 U.S. currency brought about $2 in Hong Kong bills, and when these were changed into the silver coins current in the Canton Province, we got another small premium. My parents were supplying me with $25 a month at that time and it brought me about $52 in silver currency. With the low prices at that time, this was more than ample for my needs. But by 1919 the rate of exchange had dropped to the point where an American dollar wasn't worth a dollar of the silver coin.

God knows all about the exchange rate. Nothing is too hard for Him. He was blessing my parents' store and had enabled them to secure a new location with a double front. He increased their business and they were then able to give $50 a month, which took care of the loss in exchange. When Miss Jackson's share in supporting the work was withdrawn because of her ill health, the Lord used my folks to supply $250 each month for the support of the work as a whole. This just barely met the needs, but it kept things going. We learned to look to the Lord for everything.

About this time, Mother was going through some old accounts at the store and felt impressed to dedicate to the Lord all those two years old or more, praying that He would touch hearts and cause the debts to be paid. He began to work at once and during the following months an average of nearly $50 a month was paid in and forwarded to China above the usual amounts sent. One man from Los Angeles who had cashed a bad check three years before and had never been heard from since, came in with the money and $5 extra. When the rate of exchange came bouncing back to normal in 1921, there was ample for expansion of the work: opening new outstations, sending young men to the Alliance Bible School in Wuchow, purchasing land for building some much needed buildings in Koon Shan, etc.

Once in writing home I remarked that surely in all the United States there must be other families like mine who could send their son or daughter to the foreign field and then stand behind them financially. Why don't we see more such families?

CHAPTER FIVE

Hebron Mission, Inc.

* * *

E ven during the years of shortage the Lord had been giving us visions of an enlarged work. One time this vision seemed so clear to me that I wrote home about it. The letter was barely mailed when I received a letter in which Mother said that the Lord had been speaking to them about making plans for enlarging the work. The coincidence was so striking that we were sure that the Lord's hand was in it.

We needed property and buildings to replace the rented Chinese houses in which we had begun, but according to international law only corporations, not individuals, could acquire property in areas other than the treaty ports of China. So, after much prayer, Hebron Mission, Inc. came into being in December 1920, incorporated under the laws of California.

Next, word came about a prospective new missionary, a young woman graduate from Moody Bible Institute. A few months later we heard that the Rev. Joseph Flacks, a Hebrew-Christian, was coming for a special short-term spiritual ministry among the believers in the outstations. When we received this news, we were overjoyed: to think that our great God had the work in our insignificant corner so on His heart that He was planning things like this for us!

39

But we couldn't just sit still and let our cup run over; we had to be up and doing. The little Chinese house where I'd been living could be made ready for the new missionary to share with me. But it couldn't possibly be stretched to house Mr. Flacks and the couple who would come with him. We would have to find a piece of ground where we could build a suitable house. We laid the matter before the Lord, confident that He who was sending the helpers would provide the place for them.

Within a few days a piece of land right at the foot of the mountain was offered for sale. It was above danger of flooding and was large enough for two or three houses and a garden besides. The price agreed on after bargaining was $430 in silver coin. We paid down the customary deposit of $40, the balance to be paid one month from that date. A few days afterward the owners came to us and said they'd changed their minds. They didn't want to sell. They brought with them $80 (double the amount of the deposit, as the custom was) and tried to persuade us to accept it and set them free from the promise to sell. We were sure it was God's plan for us to have that particular piece of land, so we refused. We learned on the side that someone else had offered them $600 for the land, so they wanted to sell to him.

Day after day they came, trying to persuade us to accept the double deposit money. They told us that the land would do us no good, for we would have no access to it from the downtown area. The alley which led to the northeast corner of the lot belonged to the big idol temple next door and the temple authorities wouldn't let us use that path. The alley at the northwest corner passed right in front of the Buddhist nunnery and the nuns wouldn't let us pass in front of their door because we were Christians. But still we were confident that God had a way, so we continued to refuse.

Then one day they told us it was all right. We could have access to the property by either alley we might choose. What had happened?

Political unrest developed in the province; the people wanted to oust the incumbent governor, but he controlled the military power. Since the people were afraid of possible skirmishes, the riverboats to Canton had stopped running. The would-be purchaser had his money in Canton and without the boats running he couldn't get it and had withdrawn his offer.

But our money was also in the bank in Canton, and without the boats running how would we get it to pay on the specified date? Our confidence was still in the God who performed the impossible. As the day drew near, we heard a rumor that one of the river boats was going to make a trial run to Canton. A Bible woman, Kwai Che, and I agreed that we should be on that boat. Many argued against it because of the danger of fighting or of attack by robbers. But we were confident it was the thing to do.

It was already three o'clock in the afternoon on the day of the trial run when the boat arrived in Canton—not at the usual landing on the waterfront, but at a secluded spot in a suburb about two miles from the city proper. Everyone was told to disembark there.

Kwai Che and I hired a "sampan" to take us to Shameen where the American bank was located. When we got there it was just a few minutes before four o'clock. We found the side door unlocked and went in.

The man who came to the window was a stranger to me. When I presented my check, he rather coldly reminded me that I should have come earlier, for it was then past banking hours. I explained that I'd been on the way since early morning, had only just arrived, and must get back on the boat that night, for it would be leaving very early in the morning. I told him that we were buying a piece of

41

property and that we had only one more day before the deadline for the final payment. He took my check into the manager's office and after a few minutes came back and gave me the cash in Hong Kong currency. This, then, had to be taken to the money changers in the city to be converted into silver 20-cent pieces. These were rolled into tight, paper-wrapped rolls of ten dollars each (50 coins to the roll).

After having supper at a shop where relatives of the Bible woman worked, we prepared for our return to the boat. Because of the danger of robbery, we didn't dare carry the money in our little hand baggage. We put it into money belts and strapped it around our waists. In those days there was still a certain chivalry among robbers; they didn't search the persons of women, so we were making it as safe as we knew how. We had $500 between us; I had 27 rolls strapped in two money belts around me (which must have weighed 16 pounds).

We hired a "sampan" to take us back to the boat tied up there in the suburb. Twice on the way a harsh voice out of the darkness halted us, but we were allowed to pass.

All night long, people boarded the riverboat, bringing trunks of valuables with them. If robbers had attacked, they would have gotten a lot of loot. But God was watching over us; He wanted that piece of property to be used for His glory and He protected our money for its purchase.

The building of the new house began. It wasn't ready for the new missionary, Pauline Thiers, when she came in the fall of 1920, but it was ready by the time Mr. Flacks arrived for his ministry in the spring. Writing home, he called it "The Happy Home of the Happy Ones."

The Lord blessed Mr. Flacks' ministry. He held special meetings in the eight market towns where we had preaching halls, as well as in Koon Shan and another town where there was a group of Christians. His messages were rich

food from the Word of God for the Christians at the day
meetings and a clear Gospel call in the evenings to the
crowds who packed the preaching halls. Souls were saved
and the Christians were revitalized. Before he left he
baptized seven men, most of whom had accepted the Lord
in his meetings.

One of these was Kaai Meng, an old man of 60, a mason
who had worked on building our house. We had always
invited the men who worked on our buildings to come and
hear the Gospel. Some had come and some hadn't. Kaai
Meng came frequently, but had never been willing to stay
and let anyone speak with him personally.

One evening he came to the weekly prayer meeting. The
prayer meeting began in the usual manner: an opening
song or two, a prayer, a reading from the Bible, a few
words of exhortation, a few requests for prayer; and then
all knelt to pray. After the usual two or three had led in
prayer, there was a little silence and then it was broken by
a strange voice. It was Kaai Meng's voice. He was saying,
"O God! Have mercy on me a sinner, a sinner of 60 years!
Have mercy, for Jesus' sake!"

As we rose from our knees, Kaai Meng's face was
shining. God had indeed had mercy. The Christian brothers gathered around him to rejoice with him, and the
sisters, standing at a respectful distance, smiled their
happiness. At once he wanted to know where he could buy
a Bible. We assured him that we would get one for him
from Canton as soon as possible. When he got his Bible, he
carried it with him wherever he went, to work, to meetings, and to the teahouse. Some of his old pals were
inclined to tease him about it, but he told them with a
beaming face that he was happier over the Bible than if he
had picked up a thousand dollars on the street.

Kaai Meng's testimony was backed up by such a changed
life that a fellow workman, Hoh Kui, became interested.

He was so addicted to gambling that he found it hard to keep a coat on his back, even in cold weather. He was now 40 years old and had never saved up enough money to get married. He had an old widowed mother back in his home village whom he ought to be supporting, but instead he would occasionally go home to see if he could get some piece of clothing from her to sell to pay a gambling debt. The more he listened to the Gospel, the more he was convinced that he needed it. Finally, one evening while Mr. Flacks was speaking, he said "Yes" to the pleading of the Holy Spirit and opened his heart to the Lord Jesus.

As soon as it was convenient he went home to his village to see his mother. When she heard his voice at the door she steeled her mind for what was ahead. But he came into the house with a cheery voice and a happy smile. To her surprise she saw he was wearing a respectable-looking coat.

"What's happened?" she asked. "You're different."

"Yes, I'm different," he replied. "I now believe in Jesus and He has made a new man of me." And he went on to tell her what he could about his newfound Lord. As soon as he found a place in Koon Shan where she could live, he took her there so that she could hear the Gospel for herself.

While Pauline Thiers was attending the language school in Canton, it seemed as though I simply had to have a helper of some sort. The work to be done was overwhelming: boys' and girls' schools, orphanage, industrial work, office work, besides villages and outstations. I loved it all, but one person couldn't be everywhere at once.

The Lord knew the need and brought Miss Sylvia Bancroft who had been with another mission in Canton for a few years and had a working knowledge of Cantonese. A kindred spirit, she could supervise the schools and orphanage.

44

By the spring of 1922, my parents were writing that it was time for me to come home again. I had been back on the field only three years since taking Miss Jackson home, but when the "Board" says "Come home," it's best to cooperate. And besides, there was a little hint that Mother might come back with me in the fall. Father didn't enjoy traveling very much (he wasn't a good sailor) but Mother loved to go places.

Sylvia Bancroft would be in charge of the work while I was away. During the last days before my departure, she and I were so busy that we didn't have time to sit down and go over various items she ought to know about. On the last night we went to my office determined to go through everything, even if it took all night. Finally we came to the end at four o'clock in the morning!

I had planned on having a hot bath before going to bed and then getting up at five o'clock to have breakfast and catch the early boat. I saw a light in our housekeeper's room, so very apologetically I asked, "Ah Sui, is there possibly any hot water at this hour of the night?"

"Oh, yes," she replied in her usual cheerful voice. "I have been poking the fire off and on all night to have it ready for you." Dear faithful Ah Sui! When they give out the crowns in Glory Land, she will have a beautiful one. (She is there already, but I think the giving of the crowns will wait until we all get there.)

I had the hot bath, that is, the Koon Shan version of one. Our bathroom was a partitioned corner of our upstairs porch which had a tiled floor and a drain. A basin of hot water was set on the floor with a low stool beside it.

After the bath I put on my Western clothes and caught the boat shortly after six in the morning. When the little motorboat arrived at Siu Tong where it made the connection with the railroad, we were amazed to learn that no trains were running. They had all been commandeered by the military. I simply had to get to Canton that day, since I was scheduled to speak in a Chinese church in Hong Kong the following Sunday. My ship was sailing on Monday. The Bible woman, Kwai Che, was going with me, and we just looked at each other.

"You know we've always talked about walking to Canton together some day," she said. "It looks as though this is the day. It's only 20 miles along the railroad tracks."

By that afternoon my eyes were heavy with drowsiness. It was all I could do to keep them open wide enough to watch the railroad ties as they slipped behind us. We spent the night with friends, caught the morning train for Hong Kong and the ship to America.

CHAPTER SIX

Two Mothers

* * *

The summer of 1922 at home brought any number of opportunities to witness to women's groups of all denominations. Adding a keen sense of personal happiness, though, was the fact that Mother was planning to go back with me. She would see for herself the Chinese Christians and the places known only through my letters: the church building, the house for which she and Father had sent the money, and the orphanage building.

When we arrived in Koon Shan she was surprised at the size of the structures their comparatively small gifts had produced. She looked into the happy faces of the Christian men and women and heard their cheery greeting, "Ping On" (Peace). She went a little way up the side of the mountain behind our house and looking out could see for miles to the northeast, north, and northwest. In the far distance there was a line of hazy blue mountains. The fertile, delta plain was thickly dotted with 90-odd villages and interlaced with winding waterways. The villagers had no other Christian witness than our own. She visited our nine outstations, walking with me and a Bible woman along granite slab paths to a few of the nearer ones and riding in a little covered rowboat to those more distant.

In place after place, she was welcomed by the Chinese Christians. They revered her for her gray hair and loved her for the fact that she had given her daughter to live and work among them.

On the other hand she was a real blessing to each of us, especially to me. Shortly after she left to go home, I wrote to her:

> I also pray the Lord for His grace that I may always be loving, gentle, and patient. You know my short-comings and failings, Mother dear, and I have been grateful to you over and over again for your speaking to me that day about my tone of voice. I am trusting the Lord for victory in this day by day and He is helping me.

Mother's faith grew through what she saw and heard. Writing about it, she said:

> There is a Bible woman called Ng Sham, known as the woman with the happy face. She was walking one day along the stone path between two villages singing a Gospel song because her heart was happy. A woman working the field near the path stopped her and said, "Why do you look so happy? I have nothing to make me happy; I am very miserable." What an opportunity to tell the Gospel story and to bring this poor woman into the peace and joy which comes only by believing in Jesus. Ng Sham went about with Ruth and me a great deal and her faithful witnessing to all who would listen was an inspiration to me. I wonder how many of us go about with such happy faces that unbelievers notice it and desire to know what it is that gives us happiness?

Ng Sham had been the first one to become a Christian when Miss Jackson worked in Koon Shan. When she had found peace in the Lord herself, she led her widowed sister, Mo Tak, to accept the Savior. When they returned to their native village, they were not slow to tell their parents about their new faith. The father received the preaching of the Cross with thoughtful, quiet approval, later coming to Koon Shan time and again to hear more of the Good News. He recalled a dream he had in his youth: in a time of severe illness, he had seen a Shining One come to him and draw a cross on his head, and he was healed. Now he believed that Shining One was the Lord Jesus and salvation was in His cross.

But the mother's attitude toward the daughters and their message was different. She had a stubborn disposition, and she felt it her duty to serve the ancestral tablets. If the rest of the family turned away from them to some new-fangled, "foreign devil" of religion, it was all the more her duty to remain true to the burning of daily incense.

Still another widowed sister was working at silk-weaving in the home village. Through the father she, too, was led to the Savior. In turn she led her weaving companion, the daughter of a sorcerer, to the Lord. One can imagine the stir in the village when it became known that the sorcerer's daughter had been baptized, and then had become a Bible woman.

As the father went on in his Christian life and the three daughters became workers for the Lord, the mother seemed to become more bitter. She told people that her three daughters had died. She let them know she didn't want to see them again. She composed rhymes and ditties in which she ridiculed the Gospel and slandered her daughters, singing them to visitors or to passersby in the little alley. When at last the father lay on his deathbed, she asked him if she shouldn't mortgage the house in order to have money for a real funeral with the sorcerer, priests, and their accouterments. His answer was firm, "I want none of those things; my spirit goes home to heaven. With these words he was gone.

Year after year on the anniversary of his departure, the daughters went home for a memorial service. Year after year they pleaded with and prayed for that stubborn-hearted old mother. Their younger brother, Ah Chun, became convinced of the truth in Christ Jesus, but as the only son, with a strong sense of filial obedience, he couldn't see how he could possibly oppose his mother and take his stand on the Lord's side.

At last a time came when everything seemed to go wrong: Ah Chun himself wasn't well. The responsibilities of the large estate of which he was manager seemed to be overwhelming. His wife and baby were sick. An unfavorable report of his son in high school in Canton had been brought to him. The old mother, now in ill health, was more exasperating than ever. Ah Chun recognized that something had to be done.

One night he was on his way to the estate when the thought came to him, "This trouble is all from the Devil; we must break from his power and turn to the true God!" He quickly returned home, climbed on a chair, and threw the ancestral tablets to the floor from their place of honor on the high shelf. In another moment, a blaze was consuming those "honorable ancestors" right there in the middle of the tiled floor.

The next morning when the old mother found out what had happened, she wanted to hire the proper sorcerer for such cases and replace the tablets with profoundest apologies to the ancestors for the rash act of her son. But Ah Chun was determined. "I will kill any man who comes to put those things back," he threatened. "We are done with the Devil and his business!" The stubborn will which had dominated the house so long scarcely knew what to do in the face of such determination on the part of her son. She took to her bed; without the tablets to serve, life was no longer worth living; she would die. She wanted to get some opium and make a quick end of it all, but no one would get it for her. She thought of hanging herself, but suddenly was so weak she couldn't rise from the bed. She could at least refuse to eat and slowly starve to death.

"Don't you dare let those dead daughters of mine

come," she commanded. But Ah Chun was desperate and his obedience flew to the winds. Secretly he sent an urgent message to his sisters. They responded immediately, arriving one at a time from the different places where they were engaged in the Lord's work. In spite of the old woman's protests, they waited on her and cared for her. They tempted her with dainty food, regardless of cost, so that she lost the idea of starving. And as they mingled prayer with loving service, the hard heart gradually relented a little. But the exterior was blunt and unyielding.

Finally one night, she had an unforgettable experience. It seemed that the Devil had her in his grip and was pressing her life out of her. Her torture and fear were beyond endurance. She called aloud for Koon Yam, the goddess of mercy. She cried to the ancestors whom she had served so long and faithfully. In her extremity there was no one to turn to except the God of her daughters. "O Heavenly Father!" she cried out. "The Devil is after me!" At this, her tormentor struck her one blow and was gone.

"Only one with great power could have saved me," she said the next morning. Day by day, in spite of the ridicule of her neighbors, her faith and trust in the Savior became more real and settled.

Not long after that there was to be a baptismal service in Koon Shan. This 82-year-old woman came to stay with her daughter, Ng Sham, for a few days. She gave her testimony before the church, confessing her years of darkness and sin and giving glory to the Lord Jesus for the wonderful change He had worked in her heart. A radiant smile lit up her wrinkled features as she followed her Lord in baptism.

During the year that followed Mother's visit, there were political changes and conditions of unrest. Miss Pauline Thiers left in 1922 to go work in Chefoo, where the climate was not so trying as in South China. She left behind a small local Bible school which she had begun while with Hebron Mission. We knew it was important for Chinese Christians to be sharing the Gospel with other Chinese, rather than their receiving it only from foreigners. So when some young person said he wanted to study the Bible, we had our own school in which to "try out" his seriousness about studying. This was much cheaper than trying to send him off to a boarding school elsewhere, before his earnestness for Bible study had really been well-tested.

It was my plan to visit at least one of the outstations a week, thus making the rounds of them all every two months, though now danger of robbers was considerable. One time I was coming home from Tan Tso on a small motorboat. Suddenly shots were fired from the riverbank. In less time than it takes to tell, all the passengers were flat on the floor of the boat while bullets whizzed over us or splashed in the water. The shooting had been done, it was found, not by robbers, but by men who had a grudge against that particular boat line.

Another time I went with a Bible woman to Taai Ping. The lease on our preaching hall there would soon expire and I had received word to come and look at an available building. We had only just arrived at the preaching hall when I saw a man with hatred and murder written on his face and a pistol in his hand steal quickly past the door. Suddenly there were loud shots, and people scurried in every direction. Someone beat a brass gong and the town gates and shop doors were slammed shut. We praised the Lord that we had got safely inside the preaching hall before the shooting began.

After the shooting had stopped, we waited a little while and then ventured out to go to the available building at the other end of the town. The streets were deserted except for the men with guns and they advised us which ways to avoid. So we dodged in and out around buildings until we came to the other end of the town where everything was calm except for the fact that the big heavy gates at the upper end of the street were closed and locked. Fighting of this sort had been going on almost every day since government soldiers had been taken away about a week earlier. As soon as they had gone some men opened gambling houses in almost every vacant building. Another group didn't like to see these fellows making all the money, so they too opened gambling houses. The business rivals were fighting it out in the streets.

About that time there was strife between two armed factions in the city of Tsz Tung. Fires were set in different sections, and homes and shops were plundered. The Bible woman and I felt we must go to see our workers there, taking them some warm clothing since theirs had been stolen. Things were so unsettled that no boats were running. Even the covered rowboats wouldn't venture out on the river in that area. The only way was to walk the ten miles. People told us it wasn't safe and advised against our going, but we felt that the Lord had put it on our hearts to go and He would be with us. Our elderly co-workers were so grateful for the warm clothing that we felt well repaid for going.

In Koon Shan we were awakened about four o'clock one morning by the beating of a gong and the barking of dogs. We saw a bright glow in the sky to the east. One of our men quickly went out our back gate and a few steps up the hillside to ascertain its location. In a moment he was back with the word that the fire was in the street where a Christian shoemaker lived and had his shop. The water-carrier, school cook, bigger boys and a missionary who was temporarily with us left to help carry rolls of leather and personal possessions up to our house. From the hillside we watched the progress of the fire: flames were coming out

53

of the roof of one shop while thick smoke came from the adjoining building. Then flames broke through the smoke and another shop was on fire. Step by step, shop by shop, the fire moved down the street. Could the sweating, panting carriers get the most important things from our brother's shop before the flames reached him? Suddenly the flames were less bright. A little breeze had come up and was turning the fire back. It flickered and went out just three shops before reaching the shoemaker's. On three sides of the devastated area were homes of Christians, none of which suffered loss.

CHAPTER SEVEN

The Bitter with the Sweet

*　　*　　*

Shortly after I came to China in 1915, a little girl about nine years old, Lo Tak, had been brought to me with the request that I take her to raise as my own. Her parents were not living and her relatives didn't want her because both hands were deformed. Her left arm was quite normal to the wrist, but there it divided into just two fingers. The right arm was normal only to the elbow and from there it tapered down to one finger, ending about where the wrist should have been. It seemed impossible to refuse the request, and I took her into my heart and home. She was quick to learn and did well in school. It was amazing what she could do with those three fingers! She could sew, embroider, write acceptable Chinese characters. She seemed to respond to the Gospel message and to our loving care for her.

But then a time came when she had uncooperative spells that were distressing. We tried to pray and love her through them and sometimes she responded. At last she decided to go home to her relatives. I wrote to my mother in February, 1924:

The things she said almost broke my heart, for it revealed the awful condition she is in. I very seriously doubt whether she has any real knowledge of salvation. She has it all in her head, but I fear her heart knows very little, if anything, of the saving grace of the Lord.

It seemed almost more than I could stand to think that this girl who had been here eight and a half years should now be leaving without being saved. Mother, dear, you must pray for me, things like this make me fear that my work must be nothing but wood, hay and stubble. As I look back over the work of the past years, all I can say is that I am an unprofitable servant.

Two months later I had gained some perspective.

I guess that when I wrote the letter about Lo Tak, I must have been feeling rather discouraged for the moment and I showed it in my letter. But it was really only for the "moment," for the Lord wonderfully comforted me and I felt quite all right about it all in just a short time.

The thought that the Lord Jesus Himself had so many things to discourage Him had never occurred to me in just that way before, but it is a good thought and I will store it up against future temptations to discouragement. The Devil would surely get us down and out if he possibly could. It seems sometimes as though he were working tooth and nail and it keeps one so everlastingly on the watch that when tired and worn out, you let down just the least little bit, and then everything goes wrong and you want to crawl away into a little hole where no one will ever bother you again and you won't have to carry responsibility. But then right there in that little hole you find that you are doing just what the devil wanted you to do, so in trying to get away from him and everything, you have run right into his trap.

Sometimes I feel like Elijah under the juniper tree and I all but say, "Lord, it is enough, let me die." Then again the Lord so quickens and comforts me, that it seems as though I could never possibly be discouraged again—and by His grace, I will not! I have been learning lots of lessons during the past few months, but I have not learned them perfectly yet and have to go over and over the same thing again and again, like the boys in my English class.

I used to wonder why the Lord chose me to do this particular work and I begin to think now that it was because he wanted to teach me things He couldn't teach me anywhere else, so He put me here so I would have to see myself as I really am.

During 1924 one bright spot can never be forgotten. Three years before we had received into the industrial school a young woman for whom life held nothing; she was contemplating jumping into the river as the only way out of her dilemma. As a little child Oi To had been just one mouth too many to feed, so her poor farmer parents sold her as a household servant to a more prosperous silk-weaving family. When she was about 20 years old she developed a boil that didn't heal on her lower back. She lost weight and strength. It was considered unlucky to have a servant girl die in one's possession, so her mistress found an unscrupulous woman who would act as middle person to arrange a marriage for her. The wedding was carried out without ever consulting the "bride." When the husband's family saw how thin and weak she was, they didn't want her. They needed someone strong who could go out in the fields and help with the farm work. Consequently, on the third morning, when by custom all brides go home for a little respite before taking up their duties in their new home, she was sent back with her bill of sale.

Her former mistress received her with cursing and scolding. Why had she ever taken such an ill-fated girl into her home? They all wanted her to go away and die.

But God had another plan. There was one Christian woman in that village and God let her see the girl's tear-stained face and learn the reason for it. "Come with me to Koon Shan on Sunday," she said and got permission from her mistress to let her go. When we saw her and learned her story, we said, "Come here and make lace." The mistress even advanced a few months' board money just to be rid of her.

I took her to Canton to our friend, Dr. Todd, whose diagnosis was tuberculosis of the kidneys. Since both of them were seriously affected, he could do nothing to help her except to recommend plenty of sunshine and good food. He thought she would live about three months. Actually she lived with us nearly three years, learning about the love, comfort, and hope in knowing the Lord Jesus.

As her condition worsened we took her out of the industrial school and gave her a little mat-shed all her own just off the end of our porch. Since no one wanted to take care of her at the last (tuberculosis was the most dreaded disease of South China) I somehow found time to care for her when she got to the place where she could no longer do things for herself.

One hot night in July, she seemed so weak that I fixed a bed for myself on the porch, just a step from her mat-shed. About four o'clock in the morning I heard her stir. I went to her side to see if she wanted something. She complained of the heat. There was a big palm-leaf fan at hand and I fanned her a little. Then, suddenly, in a clear, strong voice, she sang a line or two of "What can take away my sin? Nothing but the blood of Jesus," and then "Wait, meekly wait, and murmur not." She asked me if it were daylight yet and I told her it soon would be. She said she wanted to wash her face and comb her hair in order to be ready.

"Ready for what?" I asked.

"Ready for the Lord Jesus; He is coming to take me home; don't you know?" Again she sang, "What can take away my sin? Nothing but the blood of Jesus."

By that time it was daylight and the orphan boys were

out sweeping the paths around the house. When they heard her voice so loud and clear they asked me what had happened to Oi To. They all knew the previous evening she could scarcely speak, even in a hoarse whisper. When I told them she had said the Lord Jesus was coming for her, they looked aghast. Was such a thing really real?

As the morning wore on, I scarcely wanted to leave her side, for every once in a while she had something to tell me. One thing she said was, "When I have gone, be sure to write to my sister [she had contacted an older sister in Canton while living with us] and tell her that I have gone to the Heavenly Home and am perfectly happy. Tell her to be sure to believe in Jesus and then we will see each other there."

About eleven o'clock a radiant smile suddenly lit up her poor emaciated face. She lifted both arms and beckoned, singing, "Hallelujah! Thine the glory! Hallelujah! Amen!" She seemed so radiantly happy that tears of joy came to my eyes. She turned to me and seeing the tears said, "Ma, what's the matter?"

I said, "Oi To, you looked so happy. Did you see the Lord Jesus? Or what was it?"

"I didn't see Him," she answered, "but I heard His voice calling me and I saw a lot of people in white with wings and they said they had come to take me, but it wasn't time yet."

She had scarcely finished speaking when again the heavenly radiance lit up her face and her arms were raised to beckon as she sang, "Hallelujah! Thine the glory."

During the day, she gradually weakened. Occasionally she quietly sighed and said, "I am waiting for You, Lord," or "Thy will be done." Later as she lay in the coffin, the orphanage children came to look at her. Seeing the happy smile on her face, they said, "Oi To isn't dead. The Lord took her home."

CHAPTER EIGHT

Recruit from an Opium Den

* * *

Mr. and Mrs. Howard Taylor of the China Inland Mission had spent Christmas 1923 with my folks in Santa Barbara. Naturally enough, China was the favorite topic of conversation with all of them.

"Do you feel that you are going to need more missionaries for Hebron Mission?" was one of the Taylors' questions. They went on to tell of the work of Sister Eva of Friedenshort in Germany, of the fine Spirit-filled young women, Lutheran deaconesses, who were trained under her spiritual leadership, of the consecrated service that many of these deaconesses were giving in some of the China Inland Mission stations in China. They suggested that Hebron Mission apply for two of these young women.

Both Mrs. Taylor and Mother wrote to Sister Eva about the matter. It was made the subject of three days of prayer in Friedenshort and the decision was that two women should be given for the work in Koon Shan.

In the meantime, the Lord had brought to the attention of my parents a consecrated young woman, Miss Aurora Fluker, a graduate of the Bible Institute of Los Angeles and a capable office worker. Knowing the tremendous burden of correspondence and bookkeeping that I was carrying, my parents sent Miss Fluker to Koon Shan in the

61

fall of 1924 to do the secretarial work.

During her first winter, at a conference for the Chinese preachers and Bible women, she presented through an interpreter the methods of Bible study she had learned at the Institute. One of the men, Mr. Lei Sing Shau, took careful notes and then began studying the Bible according to these systematic methods. It became a new book to him and his ministry was revolutionized. His studies of Paul's Epistles helped many of the Christians in the outstations in succeeding years. Instead of being an ordinary country preacher, he became an outstanding Bible student. The story of his conversion is equally outstanding.

Years before, his uncle sent him on a business matter to their home village about ten miles into the mountains. Mr. Lei wasn't feeling very well and didn't like the thought of the long walk and the steep climb up mountain trails. A friend suggested, "Just take a puff of opium and it will give you so much pep, you won't find it a hard walk at all."

"Oh, no! I don't want to start anything like that," Lei replied.

"One puff won't make a habit," said the other.

So Lei tried it and got so much pep that he tried it on other occasions when he had something hard to do. Soon he was addicted and then his problem was to get enough money to supply his craving. He decided to run an opium den in Luk Po, living off the proceeds of selling the drug to others. He seldom went home to his wife and little girl, even though they lived in the same town. Lying on his opium bed with his cronies, he would sometimes stroke his pipe affectionately and say, "This is my best friend."

In those days two dollars a month would supply rice, vegetables, and occasionally a bit of fish or meat. But Lei by then required two dollars a day for opium. Periodically he would come to a point where he didn't have the few cents necessary for a meal of rice and vegetables. Then he would remember that his wife who worked long hours in the fields had rice. And he would go home about the time she fixed the morning meal.

When he arrived he wouldn't speak to his wife or even appear to see her. He would go straight to the kitchen and help himself to a generous portion of rice and salt fish. Then he would go without speaking to his wife or little girl, leaving them the scraps.

The shop across the street from Lei's opium den had been unoccupied for some time. One day the place was thoroughly cleaned and whitewashed inside and out, windows were repaired, and benches moved in. A sign was put up over the door, "Fook Yam Tong" (Gospel Hall). "So that's what it is," thought Mr. Lei and his cronies. "Well, we don't want any of that foreign religion."

Mr. Cheung, who had come to take charge of the Gospel Hall, had a strong, clear voice. He preached every evening, and during the daytime on Sundays and market days. Because the street was no more than 15 feet wide, his voice could be easily heard by the men in the opium den. Gradually Mr. Lei found himself becoming interested. The message denounced his sins but it offered something better. Sometimes he would stand at the door of his den. At other times he even crossed the street to stand by the door of the Gospel Hall to listen. But go in and sit down? Oh, no! It was commonly reported that Christians put something on the benches in the preaching hall so that if one sat down there he would most certainly become a believer! One day, however, when the meeting was over and everyone else had gone, Mr. Lei walked right into the Gospel Hall and spoke to Mr. Cheung.

"Can that Jesus you talk about really do something for a man like me?"

"Of course He can," Mr. Cheung answered and went on to explain how Christ died on the cross for our sins and rose again, that He is alive today with power to deliver from the bondage of sin those who sincerely trust Him.

Lei knew he was a sinner and he desperately wanted to be delivered. The two men knelt. Mr. Cheung prayed a short, earnest prayer and Lei followed with a cry to God for mercy and deliverance in Jesus' name. He got up from his knees, walked back across the street, and picked up his opium pipe. Going to the back door, he got a little hatchet and split his pipe from end to end.

His cronies saw what he was doing and cried out in horror, "Lei! Lei! Whatever are you doing? You've always said that pipe was your best friend. Is that the way to treat a good friend?"

"I've found another Friend, the Lord Jesus Christ. He is far better than this old thing. I'll have nothing more to do with this!"

Lei thought he could continue to sell opium for a living, even though he himself no longer took it. But he soon found that this wasn't pleasing to his new Lord. His patrons started going elsewhere, perhaps to get farther away from that Gospel Hall and its influence. A temporary job was offered him which helped out for the time being.

About that time he decided to test the Lord for himself to make sure that God really does answer prayer. It was a secret prayer. No one was to know anything about it except God. If the answer came, he would know for sure that God had heard him. So he prayed something like this: "God, if You see that I am a really true believer, then please let me have the privilege of going out to sell Gospel portions as a colporteur for just one month—no longer—one month is enough."

At the beginning of the following month Mr. Cheung, the preacher from the Gospel Hall, went down to Shui Hing to see Mr. Burtt and report on the work. While there Mr. Burtt said to him, "I have received a letter from a lady in America who sends a few dollars and says she wants to support a colporteur for month. She is sorry she can't send more but hopes that someone will be willing to do this work for one month. Do you suppose that in the town where you work there might be someone who would be willing to go out selling Gospel portions for one month?" Mr. Cheung thought perhaps there might be someone, so he took the few dollars and a box of books with him to his station.

That night after the evening meeting he told the story to Mr. Lei who listened quietly until the end, though the smile on his face got broader all the time. "Do you know anyone who would like the job?" Mr. Cheung asked.

"I do! I am the man! This is God's answer to my prayer." Then he told how he had asked the Lord for this very thing. The two of them marveled together at how the Lord had timed it all. Actually, the Lord had evidently told the lady in America to write her letter even before Lei had prayed. To him it was proof that the great God in Heaven hears the humble request of a newborn child of His on earth. He went out selling Gospel portions for a penny apiece in villages where the Gospel had never been preached. He took with him one of his former cronies who had also decided to follow the new way of life.

CHAPTER NINE

National Pride and Prejudice

* * *

The two young women from Germany arrived in January 1925. Sisters Margarete Seeck and Marie Luise von Mengersen were wholly consecrated to the Lord and His service, no matter what it might involve. They were a warmly welcomed addition to the little missionary family in Koon Shan. Differing nationality was of no consequence. German, American, and Chinese could work together for the Kingdom of God. Nor was the difference of denomination considered important. Lutheran, Methodist, Episcopalian, and Presbyterian could join in bringing the knowledge of salvation to those who had never heard of the Savior.

During the spring months there had been quite a bit of correspondence between Hebron "home base" in Santa Barbara, Shanghai, and Koon Shan. The Rev. G. W. Gibb, then China Director of the China Inland Mission, and his wife had visited my parents the previous year. Now they were asking me to visit them at their headquarters in Shanghai which the Hebron Home Board encouraged me to do. With the two German Sisters hard at work on language study, Aurora Fluker ably taking care of the office work and Sylvia Bancroft in charge of the schools and orphanage, it looked as though I might be able to get away for a little while. The first two weeks in May I made a quick trip to the outstations, visiting all 11 of them in 13 days. I was traveling and preaching practically every day. Strenuous? Yes, but oh, so happy!

Near the end of May, anti-foreign riots suddenly broke out in Shanghai while I was there. For days it was considered unsafe for foreigners to be seen on the streets. I stayed on the C.I.M. compound and had plenty of time to get caught up on sleep. As things began to quiet down, I ventured out to the steamship offices one day and found that a ship was sailing for Hong Kong on the very day that I had planned in the back of my mind to start for Koon Shan. I booked passage on it at once. The Gibbs urged me to stay longer, but I told them I felt it was God's time for me to leave.

In Hong Kong enroute back I found that an anti-British strike had been called by all the Chinese labor unions. Chinese were leaving the city by the thousands. I saw some friends and mentioned that I was going to Canton by the "night boat." Their quick reply was, "Well, if you are going by the night boat, you had better hurry up and get on board now or you won't be able to get on." It was still before noon, but I took their advice, only to find there were no rooms available.

"There is just one chair left," the attendant said.

"Good! I'll have that," I replied. I knew the Lord had held it for me.

In Canton the streets were full of people, mostly from labor unions and student groups, carrying banners with anti-foreign slogans. I left my suitcase and bundle with friends on the waterfront and made my way to the Shameen, expecting to see the American Consul and possibly cash a check at the bank. Since I was too early for office hours I sat on a bench under the trees beside the river. The calm of the river and the sunshine seemed a strange contrast to the noise and hubbub of the streets I had left behind me. It was a good time to "Be still and know that I am God."

When office hours arrived, I found that the bank was closed for the day. The consulate was open, but the American consul seemed very grave. An anti-foreign demonstration was planned for that very day. He strongly advised that I not try to go anywhere, not even leave Shameen, but book a room at the Victoria Hotel. I thanked him for his advice but made no promise as to what I would do.

As I walked out of the building, my heart was crying out to God, "Show me what to do!" Before I reached the outside path, everything in me was urging, "Go home to Koon Shan!" I left Shameen by the West Bridge where a British guard opened the big iron gate for me.

I had no money, but in my purse I had a postal money order payable at the post office in Canton. It had come from Singapore in a letter forwarded to me from Koon Shan while I was in Shanghai. It was the first and only time in all my years in China that I ever received money that way. God knew I would need it that day in Canton and He saw to it that I had it. I had to pass the post office on my way to the place where I had left my baggage, so I stopped in and cashed it. Within an hour and a half, the train pulled out with me on board. I was "on my way rejoicing," headed for Koon Shan. What a relief to escape from the tense turmoil of the city streets.

It was not until the next afternoon that I learned what had happened. A three-mile-long procession, composed of groups of labor union men and group of schoolchildren and soldiers started a long protest march along the waterfront. For about a mile the procession faced Shameen, separated from it merely by a narrow canal. For the most part, it was an orderly procession. Occasionally slogans were shouted or patriotic songs sung. But the French and

British on Shameen were tense with apprehension. Suddenly, somewhere, a shot was fired. The British thought, "This is it!" and opened up with machine-gun fire on the procession. They seemed oblivious to the fact that those who were passing Shameen at the time were schoolchildren, and they mowed them down by the dozens.

It was a terrible massacre and of course put the British just that much more in the wrong in the eyes of the Chinese. Everyone in the Victoria Hotel was hurried onto a British gunboat and sent off to Hong Kong. It was months before they could get back. How thankful I was that I hadn't taken the American consul's advice that day and gone to the hotel!

Back in Koon Shan everything was still quiet. The people knew us. There were no labor unions or student protests. We had no trouble buying food. But gradually the atmosphere even in Koon Shan became more and more charged with the spirit of nationalism. Love of country was put before everything else, and this implied a hatred for the foreigners who for decades had been exploiting China's resources. Two of our younger preachers who wanted to be considered patriotic were almost swept off their feet by the movement. Nothing we could say helped at all, for they felt we were merely foreigners and didn't understand how much they loved their country. So we stopped advising them and prayed earnestly to God.

At this time of need, the Lord brought a Chinese pastor named Au to work with us. All our workers knew and highly respected him. He was middle-aged, clear-sighted, and straight-speaking.

The day he arrived, a little group of Christians met him at the boat landing in Koon Shan and came with him to the church where they had planned a little reception. They asked Pastor Au to speak a short while following which there would be tea and refreshments. Pastor Au responded that he hadn't expected anything like this, but since they had asked him, he would say a few words.

He spoke for over an hour. And in his talk, he said things that our hearts had been aching to say, but hadn't been able to because we were foreigners. Pastor Au took an uncompromising stand on the authority of Jesus Christ as Head of the Church and of the life of the individual Christian. Everything else, even patriotism, must be subservient to Him. In the final analysis, only Christ could "save the country," not slogans, nor shouting demonstrators.

Another matter in which he helped was the organizing of the Chinese church. From the beginning church government had been in the hands of the missionaries. With the rise of this keen spirit of nationalism, we had realized that it was time for a change. With Mr. Lei's help we had drawn up a plan for "nationalizing" the church. Now aided by the insight and leadership of Pastor Au, these plans were finalized. The first meeting of the church council, composed of representatives from the outstations and Koon Shan, was held early in 1926. A constitution was drawn up and adopted. The governing power was in the hands of the Chinese church, and missionaries served on the committee only as they were elected to various offices by the Chinese church. Relations between the Chinese Christians and missionaries had always been amicable, so the new form of government did not mean any break, but rather a closer welding together of the local national church and the foreign missionaries.

CHAPTER TEN

The House on Cheung Chow Island

* * *

A lthough we were safe in Koon Shan from the dangers caused by the anti-foreign boycott, there were definite inconveniences. The most serious was getting our checks cashed. The American consul warned that it was dangerous for foreigners to be seen on the streets in Canton, and strongly advised us not to come in person. Although the banks on Shameen were open for business, no Chinese could pass the picket lines to go there. Our good friend, Dr. Todd, however, had a friend in the Customs office who had access to Shameen by a motorboat attached to an American gunboat anchored in the river. So we sent our checks to Dr. Todd by mail, waited a few days, and then sent one of our Chinese helpers to Dr. Todd to get the cash.

That was the first summer in China for the German sisters and Aurora Fluker. By rights they ought to get away to the coast for a change from the sticky humidity of Koon Shan. Finally by the end of August, it was considered safe enough for them to go through Canton on their way to Hong Kong if they wore sleeve bands clearly marked with large Chinese characters indicating that they were "German" or "American." The boycott ended in October 1926, more than a year later.

In the meantime, although conditions in the country

were unsettled, Pastor Au and I held special meetings in one outstation after another.

We were unwilling to let "unsettled conditions" keep us from going out in our area with the Gospel. I was repeatedly warned not to go to different places lest bandits kidnap me, but as I prayed about the matter, I felt assured that the Lord was just as able to protect me in other places on His business as He was to keep me safe while I was at home. So I continued to go and I never was molested.

In the spring of 1926, friends visited us from the Canton Christian College (which later became Lingnan University). One of them, Mr. R. D. McDermott, told of their visit in a circular letter written to his friends at home:

At 1:30 we arrived at Koon Shan, which lies snugly at the foot of Sai Chiu Mountain. A coolie carried our baggage and directed us to the Hebron Mission. We had sent a letter one day in advance of our departure, but it evidently hadn't arrived yet, judging from the surprised attitude of the folks at the mission, who hadn't had but one other foreign visitor in the course of a year. We were really on the missionary frontier in China.

As we passed through the streets of the city on our way to the mission, it seemed as if I could notice a difference in the faces and the manner of the people as they greeted us foreigners. Afterward as I became better acquainted with the missionaries of this station and with their splendid work, I was able to understand why the Chinese here have a more friendly and brotherly attitude toward foreigners than one sees in many other places in China. In these times of bitter anti-Christian and anti-foreign feeling, it was encouraging to see how this little band of five staunch Christians (all women) have the respect and goodwill of this city of about 20,000 people.

In the mission compound we found two very ordinary buildings; one the home of the missionaries, the other a primary school for girls and for the training of Bible women. These trained Chinese Bible women do work in the ten outstations, all of which are located in market towns not more than a day's journey away.

The Hebron Mission is doing two things among this class of people. They have an industrial school for girls where they can learn to do something else besides reel silk. Here they may learn cloth-weaving and lacemaking and attend the evening school where they learn to read. Even though the girls have no money they may enter this school and be paid a sufficient wage for their livelihood while learning. It also has a splendid, but modest, church building in the heart of the city with a Chinese pastor and a membership of about 140. Through their schools, the church, and personal evangelism, they are doing much to bring new light and hope into the lives of these oppressed people.

I attended the weekly prayer service at the little church. There were twenty-five women, five girls, ten men and five boys in attendance. The Pastor began the service by reading a chapter from the New Testament. Men and women eagerly arose to testify for what Christ had done for them. Then followed a long session of prayer. I couldn't understand a word that these people were saying, but somehow by the fervor of their voices I was made to share their sorrows and joys in Christ Jesus. Never before had Christ seemed so near and I almost believed I could reach out my hand and touch Him. Never before had I seen so clearly His work among needy people.

A further evidence of the hand of God working among these people is the dispelling of evil spirits from certain demon-possessed persons who have come to the mission for help. It seems queer in this age to speak of demon-possessed lives, but it so happens that some people here worship the evil spirits or evil gods until they actually become possessed with them. At times they will appear normal and then at other times they will be overcome with violent emotions, over which they have no control. A number of these people, especially women, have been so helped by prayer that they have become Bible women and they testify that the old life has left them entirely.

In the summer of 1926 we planned a vacation at the coast and rented a house on Cheung Chow Island for two months. Just before we left to return to Koon Shan a missionary friend asked if we had ever thought of buying a house there on the island for the use of our missionaries. If so, one was for sale. She pointed out No. 25 on the top of another hill a little farther west, but nearer to the village and the boat landing. In the meantime, of course, we had written home enthusiastically about the quiet restfulness of the place, the beautiful view, the lovely sea breeze, etc.

In those days it took a month for a letter to go and another month for a reply. We had been back in Koon Shan some time before we received a letter from home saying in effect: "We are so glad you have found a good place for vacation. Inquire around a little and find out if there is a house for sale there on the island; if so, we will buy it for you and give it to you for a birthday present."

Who were we, little Hebron Mission, to have a house on Cheung Chow Island? But the Lord had His plan. By the end of the year the purchase had been finalized. My parents did not know, nor did we, what this property was to mean during the years to come.

The fall was busy with special meetings in outstations. With the younger missionaries taking care of the schools, orphanage, and office work in Koon Shan, it was wonderful to be free to work in villages. I fairly reveled in the opportunity.

Tai Hing Shi, our newest outstation with only a few believers, had its meetings near the end of November. There, a blind man named Goon Tai Hing had been known as the crossest and meanest man in the village. In former years he had been a successful tailor in foreign ports, but now he had come home blind and lame as a result of a life of dissipation. His wife deserted him, going off to find work in another village, leaving him alone in their bare, earth-floor hut. Village boys delighted to stand about his door teasing and tormenting him, deftly evading the brandishing bamboo pole that augmented his curses.

When he had first come home he had $40 (Chinese silver coins) which he had placed in a rice shop and every month he received 40 cents' worth of rice.

As the years of hopeless dejection dragged on, a hunger arose in his heart for "something." He longed for someone to come and talk to him, to give him something to think about. At last, one day he received a message from his cousin saying that she had become a Christian and would send the Bible woman to tell him about the Savior. He eagerly awaited her visit. Her message of salvation, life, and hope in Christ Jesus found a ready response in his open heart. Joy and light displaced darkness and despair.

His wife occasionally came home to see whether blind Goon was still alive. On one of these visits she learned of the change that had come to her husband. He urged her to accept the Savior, but she was so embittered by grief and hardship that she wouldn't listen. Goon began to pray for her, for he had learned that God answers prayer. Two or three years went by. He felt impressed that unless some sickness came into her life she wouldn't feel her need of a Savior, and he prayed that God would deal with her as He saw best.

Finally she came home for one of her brief visits at the beginning of summer. While she was storing away the winter bedding in a little loft, she slipped and fell to the floor below, a distance of eight or ten feet. There she lay, a crippled, suffering heap and no one but a blind, lame husband to help her. Standing over her, Goon poured out his heart to God. Neighbors came and put her to bed.

For days Goon patiently and tenderly cared for his

suffering wife, with every little act of service breathing a prayer to the One who is able to save. Gradually her hard heart softened. She realized that somehow the God of her husband must be a God of power and of love and that she had been sinning against Him. Her pain lessened and her strength began to return. Within three weeks she was able to go back to her work in the neighboring village. New life and hope had sprung up in her heart.

Their son-in-law came home during the strike in Hong Kong, with no money and no work. The daughter asked for the $40 invested in the rice shop to start her husband in business selling trifles on the street. While they promised to pay interest on the money, the business didn't prosper and soon his $40 was gone. But the Lord had already put it on the hearts of several Christians to help this blind brother and, knowing his loss, they were careful to see that his needs were supplied. In those days the average poor people of our district found that at least three or four dollars were necessary for a month's expenses. Goon seemed to thrive on a dollar and a half or two dollars. In fact, he said, if he ate more, he suffered from indigestion.

The industrial school was also a cause for thanksgiving. To have a place where needy women and girls could find refuge and be led to the Lord Jesus brought joy to our hearts. A letter to my parents written in January of 1927 tells why we were so thankful the Lord had led us to open industrial work in 1916:

On the afternoon of December 30th, one of our industrial women and Ah Miu (a Bible woman) were coming home from Tai Kong Hui in a little boat. As they passed a village, someone called for the boat to stop and take another passenger. A man helped a woman into the boat, paid her fare, and told the boat-woman that she would know where to go when they reached Koon Shan. Our two women tried to converse with her, but found that she was evidently insane. Then they spoke to her of the Lord and His power to save and she grasped at the words like someone drowning.

When the boat reached Koon Shan, she insisted on following our women, saying that she didn't know the way to her home. They were doubtful as to what to do, knowing nothing about the woman. A crowd gathered quickly and everyone said, "Yes, she is crazy; take her with you; she is just the kind of a case for the Christians." So our women brought her to the industrial school.

It seems that she had been raving crazily for some time. The man who took her to the boat was her husband. He wanted to send her back to her father's home. The neighbors said he beat her all the way from his home to the boat, but she didn't remember it and couldn't account for the huge black-and-blue spots all down her limbs. The girls prayed with her and showed loving sympathy and it was only a few days before she was as sane and normal as could be.

This evening when she came to my room she said over and over again how thankful she was for the wonderful way the Lord had healed her. Her father is in Canton and she now wants to go and see him so that he, too, can see what God has done for her.

If time and space permitted I could go on with many more such stories of God's grace as demonstrated in the lives of poor and needy women. Some of our critics in the villages said that we Christians were like the junkman who goes around gathering up old broken iron or copper pots and pans to make them over into something useful. We didn't object to the criticism, for we knew that God is able to take sinful, broken lives and make them over. Several of our Bible women were living testimonies to this transforming power.

It was the spring of 1927 and the Hebron Home Board had been encouraging me to come home again. The prospect was pleasant, but I hated to leave the work and people that I loved so much. Since there were rumors of fresh anti-foreign activities I told our missionaries when I left Koon Shan that if the American consul ordered Aurora Fluker and Sylvia Bancroft to evacuate, the two German sisters were to go with them to the house on Cheung Chow Island.

As it happened, they had to evacuate, and prospects for a return to the country were not at all bright. Aurora Fluker had her correspondence and bookkeeping with her, so she was kept busy. The two German Sisters were still working hard on the language and they were occupied. But Sylvia Bancroft had had to leave her school and orphanage work behind. There was a wide open door for someone to take charge of a missionary home in Hong Kong, and she took that up. Later she went into boat mission work among the thousands of boat people in and around Cheung Chow Island. Her connection with Hebron Mission was severed, but the bond of friendship lasted down through the years.

It was 1928 before the situation finally cleared enough for the missionaries to return to Koon Shan. They found that the Chinese Christians and workers had carried on faithfully in their absence.

In the spring of 1929 Aurora Fluker came home for furlough; her health had not been good in China. In the end it seemed best for her not to return. She became a valued helper in the work of the Biblical Research Society in Los Angeles. My mother loved her as a "third daughter" and as long as she lived she was one of the family to us.

CHAPTER ELEVEN

Count It All Joy

* * *

Home brought no opportunity for idleness. Two months after my arrival, Mother's health failed and for two years she was unable to carry on her work as manager of the dry-goods store. This store, operated as a stewardship for the Lord, sent me to China and supported me there, sent out other helpers and supported them, built churches, and supported Chinese workers. It was up to me now to step in and carry on while Mother was temporarily ill.

It was a long way from evangelistic work in the villages of China to the managing of a dry-goods store in modern America. But I found that "I can do all things through Christ who strengtheneth me." I brought the problems home to talk over with Mother at noon or in the evenings and we took them to the Lord together. It helped to know that I could be a comfort to Mother in her time of need, especially when she had worked so hard for the sake of the Lord's work in China. But as weeks slipped into months and months into years, I began to be impatient to get back to China, especially after the missionaries who had had to evacuate to the house on Cheung Chow were able to return to the country. At that time the words of a hymn by W. H. Pike became very precious to me; I hummed them to myself and to the Lord as I was driving to and from work and whenever I was at leisure:

O gracious God, on Thee I wait,
With Thine own self my being fill;
As day by day my life I live,
To do Thy will, Thy blessed will.
To do Thy will, yes, that is all;
To do Thy will, obey Thy call,
To follow, Lord, where Thou dost lead,
To do Thy will is all I need.

At last the time came when Mother could be back in the store. Actually, she was as eager to be back at her work as I was to get back to China, for she had always considered it a stewardship for the Lord and she wanted to be faithful in carrying on for Him. Some well-meaning friends protested that since she was no longer young (she was 63 that year) she ought not to let me go so far away. But her reply was, "I have laid my daughter on the altar. You don't expect me to take her back, do you?"

And so in September 1929, I again set sail for China. How good it was to arrive back in Koon Shan. But it wasn't entirely without sadness, for the welcome meeting which the Chinese church gave for me was also the farewell meeting for the two German sisters who were leaving for their first furlough. They were loved by the Chinese Christians, who hated to see them go, even for the year of their furlough. Thus, as far as missionaries were concerned, I was again left alone. But actually I wasn't alone, nor did I ever feel lonely. The Lord was present and I was perfectly at home with the Chinese Christians. There were still plenty of problems, difficulties, and trials, but at home I had relearned the value of James 1: 2, "Count it all joy." It became our watchword.

Ah Sui, our faithful household cook, a Shek Waan woman whose husband had abandoned her and their little daughter, didn't know a word of English until I taught her to say, "Count it all joy." We greeted one another with it the first thing in the morning and the last thing at night and again through the day whenever anything disturbing came along.

The church council made plans for special meetings in Koon Shan and the outstations. We invited the Rev. Burtt from Shiu Hing to come for those in Koon Shan. He replied that he would come if we were willing to meet his conditions: the workers and Christians were to prepare themselves the week preceding the meetings by prayer and fasting—that was, fasting in the morning, with the first meal of the day after the prayer meeting at noon. We agreed to do this and Mr. Burtt came to us in the power of the Spirit. Hearts were melted, sins were confessed, wrongs were made right, and lives were touched. We had prayed for this through the years. Now we were experiencing it.

The first outstation to have a special meeting was Loh Hong. Would the Holy Spirit continue the work there He had begun in Koon Shan? The prospect was not too bright. Neither of the Loh Hong workers had been to the Koon Shan meetings. There was a feeling that they didn't have much sympathy for these meetings. But trusting in the Lord as my sufficiency, I went to Loh Hong a week before the meetings were to start and began the preparatory prayer and fasting meetings.

The Holy Spirit came into our midst and after about two or three days of praying, even the preacher humbly confessed his coldness and indifference. When Mr. Lei, the former opium addict, came a few days later for the Bible messages, hearts were open and hungry. In the evening meetings for the unsaved there were many decisions, especially among men who had listened to the Gospel for two or three years, but had never accepted it. After the meetings were over, Mr. Lei said that the past week had been the happiest in all his ten years of serving the Lord.

The Lord blessed the following special meetings held in several other outstations. I couldn't help but feel that the blessing was at least partly due to Mother's sacrifice in letting me be in China when she really needed my help at home.

But discouraging things also had to be dealt with. One young man resigned from the work; he seemed halfhearted for the Lord anyway, so it was perhaps just as well that he did leave. But at the same time another good man handed in his resignation. In a letter home I wrote:

> I cannot feel that it is the Lord's will for this man to leave. I told Mr. Lei that the Devil saw we were getting all fixed for a real revival throughout the church, so he thought he would get in some of his work and try to spoil things. Lei replied that the Devil was planning his own Five-Year Campaign to offset ours! But the Devil is a defeated foe and we are not going to let him get the best of us.

It was one more thing in which we could say, "Count it all joy."

But strenuous as life as with the perplexing problems that cropped up at unexpected times, plans for enlarging the work were forming in my mind. I wrote home:

> An article in the "World Dominion" magazine helped me to bring these plans to a head, I hope definitely to begin putting them into action right away. I don't think we should hold back from enlarging the work and opening up new stations merely because of a shortage of either money or men. So that article, "Practising New Testament Methods," went right to the spot with me and made me feel that we need no longer delay.

> There was another article in the same number from which I got some valuable ideas. The plan is now

84

something like this: As regards our already opened stations, this fall we will strongly emphasize their need to take over more and more responsibility for running their own affairs. This means not only in the area of finances, but also in conducting meetings, getting together for Bible study and prayer (even without the leadership of a paid worker), and learning to be soul winners. The idea is not only to emphasize this, but also to put them at it by taking the workers away for more work in the villages and their other towns. They will be thrown on their own resources, or rather, thrown on the help and guidance of the Holy Spirit.

In order to spread the Gospel to other places, a worker, perhaps with some of the Bible students, should go to Tai Tung (the market on the south side of our Sai Ch'iu Mountain) regularly once or twice a week. There they can preach in the open or wherever opportunity offers, distributing tracts and Scripture portions. Before long we expect someone to say to the worker, "Stay with me tonight; I want to hear more of what you have to say."

And that will be an opening; the worker will be expected to spend a night there, possibly once or twice a week. This first inquirer is to be made to realize that he or she should interest others and bring them in for the little Bible classes or prayer gatherings. We won't rent a building for a chapel then. The new little circle of believers must be independent from the very beginning.

This plan was later adopted by the church council. However, it was put into practice by the Koon Shan Church and workers almost as soon as it was proposed, since some of us had a real burden for the people of Tai Tung, only about two hours' walk from Koon Shan.

After our group had preached in the town market several times, I went with a Bible woman into the residence district and was invited to stay the night. What a delight to spend the evening sharing the riches of Christ with those who had never heard!

85

CHAPTER TWELVE

A Father to the Fatherless

* * *

One day when I was in Canton on a business trip, I stopped at the Hackett Hospital (Presbyterian) to collect for some mosquito nets that they had ordered from our industrial department. There I met Mrs. Hoffman, an old friend from Miss Jackson's days, who asked me to stay for dinner that evening. She was having Leland Wong, China's best known evangelist, as a dinner guest. That invitation was no "happenstance."

During the conversation I asked Mr. Wong if he ever accepted invitations to speak in little village churches (I had only heard of his speaking to large crowds in big cities). He didn't say "No" to my question, so I followed it up with a definite invitation to come to Koon Shan at the time of the next Chinese New Year, a few months away. He consulted his date book and agreed.

In February 1933, Mr. Wong came to Koon Shan for five days. He spoke twice each day and led the prayer meeting two mornings as well. Evening after evening men and women responded: the father of a boy in the day school, other men from the market, women from the neighborhood, a girl who had been weaving in the industrial department for months, and many of our orphanage children.

But two teenage boys, the son of Mr. Lei Sing Shau and

87

the younger brother of our head schoolteacher, just didn't seem to be able to yield to the pleadings of the Spirit. On the fourth night, Mr. Wong spoke on the prodigal son. He made the longing, yearning love of the Father so real that it seemed as though no one could resist. That night and the next day much private prayer was offered for the two boys. When the invitation was being given the last night and I saw that they didn't respond at first, I slipped out to the side room and pleaded with the Lord for them. When I went back in, the two boys, together with others, were standing in front of the platform.

Then Mr. Wong asked if any present wanted to dedicate their lives to the Lord for His service. One by one they came from all over the building, men and women, girls and boys. There must have been over 20 in all, including Yan Tin, the daughter of Leung Tse Shing, and her brother Fei Lik.

Yan Tin's birth had marked the conversion of her father after a strange history. Leunz Tse Shing's first two wives had died in childbirth. His third wife, a strong country woman, had given birth to Yan Tin and immediately seemed demon-possessed. Facing the loss of another wife and child, Leung was despondent. But Ng Sham, the Bible woman with the happy face, came along just then and he explained his plight. "Let me come and see her," she said. "I'll come and pray with her. The Lord will be able to save her." Just a new Christian herself, she believed that nothing was too hard for her Lord.

In the home they found the third wife sitting erect and regal on the bed, saying strange things in a strange voice. She seemed to expect to be worshiped. They had doubt that she was under the power of a demon. The baby lay off to one side, uncared for.

Ng Sham rebuked the demon in the name of the Lord Jesus Christ and prayed for His blessing on the family.

The young mother's attitude changed almost immediately. She dropped her head and began to cry. "Oh!" her husband said, "If the Devil cries when he hears the name of Jesus, then it's Jesus for me from now on."

Ng Sham continued praying for complete deliverance, while Leung took down the fetishes and good luck charms over the bed and deposited them in the excrement jars outside, the most undignified place he could think of. As she told Leung more about Jesus and His power, the mother took the baby and began suckling it.

The birth of that little girl, named Yan Tin ("Grace"), was a turning point for the family. The father gave his testimony whenever he had an opportunity and became a diligent Bible student. He had a marvelous memory for the Scriptures, including chapter and verse. Some who were demon-possessed were in turn released through his faith and prayers for them. Now, at Mr. Wong's meetings, Yan Tin and her brother were personally dedicating their lives to the Savior.

Yet just one drop was lacking in our cup. There had been no response whatever on the part of a boy who had been with us since he was just a little fellow. About two years previously he had asked for baptism, but the church thought he hadn't given evidence of salvation so he was asked to wait. That upset him and afterward he showed no interest in spiritual things. Later he developed tuberculosis and died without any outward evidence of repentance.

About this time we faced a new problem. The value of the American dollar was dropping again. We had been enjoying a time when the rate of exchange was especially good, but now every time we cashed a check we seemed to get a lower rate. The "depression" was making things hard in the States. Money was tight and trade was slack. After the Santa Barbara earthquake in 1925, my parents had bought a new location for the store, negotiating a loan from the bank in order to do so. They thought that the payments on principal and interest wouldn't be more than the rent they would have to pay on the old place when the earthquake damage was repaired. But now the bank was tightening its requirements and with the slack trade, meeting the payments was difficult. On April 9, 1933, I wrote to Mother:

A month ago when I first heard (through the Chinese newspapers) of the banks being closed, it did alarm me, but I went right to the prayer room and talked it all over with the Lord. As I got my eyes entirely on Him, off the store and rate of exchange, He gave me peace and confidence about it all.

Naturally in the following days my mind was active in planning how to cut down, if necessary. But somehow there kept coming to my mind the words: "They need not depart; give ye them to eat"; and "Why are ye fearful? oh, ye of little faith!" Well, at any rate, we will go just one step at a time—curtail, if that is what the Lord wants, or go on in faith, if that is His plan.

What worries me is that with business so desperately dull, how are you going to meet the interest payment tomorrow (the 10th of the month)? And another thing —with business so poor, it won't be possible for you to continue the $100 a month. Shouldn't we cut it to $50? Or I am thinking that I had better stop writing checks altogether and the end of each month you send a check for whatever you have to give. Unless some more hopeful word comes from you during this month, I won't plan to write a check for more than $50 or $75 the first of May; we will get along some way. The Lord is able to supply our needs and yours, too.

Before that month was over, money was sent from Germany to our two German sisters with no word of explanation about how it was to be used. Then word came from home that just before the 10th of April the store had

two such good days there had been enough money to meet
the interest payment.

In May, 36 persons were received into the church by
baptism. Ten were from Koon Shan, the rest from the outstations. Some from Koon Shan came as a result of Leland
Wong's meetings in February. On the 3rd of June I wrote
home:

When I went to Shek Waan, I took along the book,
"The Kneeling Christian." I had read it before, but its
message gripped me this time. It has made me long
and resolve to be more of a pray-er than I have been.
At a time when the financial outlook is anything but
promising, are we simply going to succumb and re-
trench, or are we going to give the Lord a chance to
show what He can do in response to believing prayer?
I am in favor of the latter course.

Although we have been what is called a faith mission,
still there has been a good deal of sight about our
faith. We have been able to see a fairly definite
amount of money come in each month from the store
and from friends. The rate of exchange has made
things look quite cheerful. But now when these
amounts cannot be counted on and the exchange rate
is uncertain, what about our faith?

Of course, it's essential that we get the mind of the
Lord on this. If for reasons beneficial to the Chinese
church, finances should be reduced, we don't want to
insist that He continue to give us as much as we have
had. But if He wants us to continue with our present
program and even push out into new work, then we
can trust Him to supply the means.

Just at this time two or three children want to come to
our orphanage. In the Old Testament, God said over
and over again that He would be a Father to the
fatherless. As I went to the Lord in prayer to ask if we
should take a sweet little tot whom I saw in Shek
Waan, almost before I had spoken the words, "Father,
what shall we do about this little one?" the answer
rang in my heart, "Suffer the little ones to come unto

91

me and forbid them not." What could I say? Then when I came back to Koon Shan, there was a little fatherless boy wanting to be received. It was the first of June and I turned the Scripture calendar to the page for that month and the picture was of the Lord Jesus receiving and blessing little children. Only a coincidence, or course, but it made me the more confident that the Lord does love and want to care for these little tots. But the big problem is room for them. Where can we put them?

CHAPTER THIRTEEN

The Benefactor of Saam Tsuen

*   *   *

Near the end of June, I received a letter from Leland Wong who said he wanted to see me about a matter of the Lord's work. He set a date for me to meet him at a Canton hotel, saying he would pay expenses for my trip. (As the boat fare from Koon Shan to Canton at that time was only about 20 cents, financing the trip was no problem.)

He had aroused my curiosity and I was there at the appointed day and hour. Mr. Wong began telling me about a friend of his with whom he had stayed while in Shanghai for evangelistic meetings. This Mr. K. S. Lee had gone to the States many years previously as a teenager and had lived with an uncle who had a restaurant. At school a friendly boy had invited him to go to Sunday school. The people at the church were nice to him so when the pastor asked if he didn't want to be baptized, he said "Yes." But he really didn't know what it meant to be a Christian. Later he graduated from Cornell University and came back to China where he eventually went into the exchange brokerage business. He did well and soon became prosperous. Though he was a member of the YMCA Board of Directors and a church officer, he never read the Bible for himself or prayed. After more than ten years of worldly living, he realized the need of being born again and had yielded to the Holy Spirit. His life had changed and now he was concerned for the people of his native village in South China. He wanted to open some sort of Christian work there.

He had approached the China Inland Mission about it, but as the Kwong Tung Province was not in their field, they had declined. He had then sent $500 to a mission in Canton, asking them to start something in his village and saying he would be financially responsible. In about a year's time, having made a trip to the village, they sent him a report of their findings. They suggested that industrial work for women and girls might be a good approach to reach the people with the Gospel. And as an example they cited the industrial work being done by our Hebron Mission.

K. S. Lee showed the report to Leland Wong and asked him what he knew about the Hebron Mission. Mr. Wong told him of his special meetings in Koon Shan at the Chinese New Year and encouraged him to think that we were the ones to open work in that needy village.

At once I thought of reasons why we shouldn't undertake it. It was not in our area either. It would probably take two days' travel by riverboat to get there. The dialect was different; our Bible women and other helpers wouldn't be able to make themselves understood. What was more, other missions were working in that area, quite near to K. S. Lee's village. According to mission etiquette, it wasn't right that we should go in there. Mr. Wong told me to write to K. S. Lee and reminded me again that K. S. Lee would pay all expenses.

I wrote the letter, stating these objections quite fully. But, I added the sentence, "If the Lord should tell me to go there to open the work, I would go, of course."

The answer quickly came back from Shanghai: "The Lord is telling you to go to my village. Come to Shanghai to talk it over with me. I will pay your travel expenses." I wrote back that I could see no sense in going to Shanghai to talk about something I knew nothing about. I would take a trip to the village, see it firsthand, and then try to judge whether the Lord's hand was in this matter.

In July 1933 I attended, as usual, the Chinese summer Deeper Life Conference in Canton. There I came into contact and fellowship with a Miss Lee, a consecrated young Chinese woman who had just completed her studies at the Alliance Bible Institute inWuchow. She was looking for the right place for summer evangelistic work. I told her of K. S. Lee's concern for his native village and after prayer we decided that we would go there together when the conference was over.

Our route took us through the treaty port of Kong Moon, where we had to spend the night and get a different riverboat the next morning. Late in the afternoon, we dropped in at the Chinese church in Kong Moon just to see if there might be someone we knew. As we entered, a young woman was coming toward the door to go out. She and my companion greeted each other with surprise and delight. They were schoolmates who hadn't seen each other for years. She was just going to leave for her field of work in the eastern part of the province and, of course, she wanted to know what had brought us to Kong Moon. We told her of the wealthy man in Shanghai who was concerned about the people of his home village, Saam Tsuen.

"Oh!" she said. "My home village is quite near Saam Tsuen and I haven't been back there for a long time. What is more, I was led to the Lord by the one Christian woman who lives in Saam Tsuen. I think I'll go with you." And so it was that we, complete strangers to the area, had for our travel companion Miss Wong, who was perfectly at home in both the area and dialect.

We got off the riverboat the next afternoon at Miss

Wong's village. A new little church had recently been built in the rice fields outside the village and we were welcomed by the preacher and his energetic wife. The building's second floor furnished excellent sleeping quarters for our little party during the day or two we spent getting acquainted with the people of the neighborhood and learning all we could about Saam Tsuen.

Except for its size, Saam Tsuen was like hundreds of other villages of South China: narrow alleys with long rows of gray brick houses joined together, a few wide open spaces with paved areas for threshing floors, plenty of room for the water buffaloes to lie and chew their cud when not plowing the surrounding fields or tramping out the harvested grain, large ponds of stagnant water (frequently refreshed by heavy rains) where buffaloes could submerge themselves when the heat or pestering flies became more than they could stand. But it was different in that it was unusually large. Some claimed that it had as many as 10,000 people. Another unusual feature was that all the men were of the Lee (Lei) clan (most villages have at least two or three clans living in them, such as the Wongs, Chans, and Fongs). Proud of their clan and village, these Lees were known as wicked, extremely cruel people.

Some of the men collaborated with a band of robbers who had their headquarters in the high mountains just to the south. People were frequently kidnapped from neighboring villages and held in Saam Tsuen for high ransom. If money weren't forthcoming, a piece of the victim's ear or finger would be cut off and sent to the relatives with the word that if they didn't pay, the victim would be further cut to pieces. With such stories common in the surrounding villages, it wasn't surprising that Christians hesitated about going to Saam Tsuen to preach the Gospel. What preacher had any means of paying ransom?

The second day after our arrival, the three of us set out

for Saam Tsuen, an hour's walk through the beautiful countryside. We went directly to where Miss Wong's friend was living. How surprised she was to have three Christians come to visit her, one a Westerner.

Her husband had gone to Canada. At first he had sent money back for her and the children, a boy and girl aged 11 and 13, but now it had been years since she'd had any word from him. It was reported among other Saam Tsuen men who had gone to Canada that he had another wife and family there. Her husband's parents had a city home in Kong Moon and she and the children had spent some time with them. While she was there she had heard the Gospel and become a Christian.

At once she consulted the pastor about what she should do to support herself and her children, and also be helpful to the people of her village. He advised her to go to Canton, take a course in midwifery, and then go into practice in Saam Tsuen. A family who wanted a midwife would usually call her early so she would have a few hours of waiting in which to tell them about what the Lord Jesus had done for her. She had taken his advice and here she was, one light trying to shine in the darkness of that village. But she was discouraged.

While listening to her story, another Voice had been speaking to my heart. "If we could send a Bible woman here, would that help?" I asked her. "Would there be a place for her to live?"

"Oh, a Bible woman would be a wonderful help!" she exclaimed. "And there is a place for her to live. The house at the upper end of the alley is the house to which I was brought as a bride; it is my house, I can do what I will with it. I shall be glad to have a Bible woman live there."

"Be patient a little longer," I encouraged her. "Keep on praying. I believe God will provide the right Bible woman."

I had committed myself. The Lord had spoken to me and told me that the work in Saam Tsuen was something He wanted me to undertake. Now for the trip to Shanghai to talk to K. S. Lee.

Mr. Lee was enthusiastic to hear that I had been to his village, trying to tell the women about the living God and agreed that the work should begin in a small way, with just a Bible woman at first. He told me that if I found any orphans there to take them to our orphanage in Koon Shan. He would pay expenses.

Not long after my return from Shanghai, I made another trip to Saam Tsuen. I took with me a woman from our industrial department who had come to us a few months previously. She was a young Christian, but she knew the Saam Tsuen dialect.

We stayed at the home of Mrs. Lee, the midwife, and day after day we went from house to house through the village, trying to tell the women about the living God and His wonderful Son, our Savior. But rarely was anyone willing to listen. Usually we were told to move on.

In the evenings at Mrs. Lee's house we had a little gathering of the neighborhood children. We told them stories from a scroll of Bible pictures and taught them little choruses. After the children had gone to bed, the women would stay longer asking questions. This message of a living, loving God was all so new to them.

One evening one of the women whispered to us that a council meeting of the village elders was being held in the ancestral hall just down the street. She thought it had something to do with us, but wasn't sure. Her husband had been called to attend. Whether or not it concerned us, we went on with our little meeting. Before the last of the women had gone, many footsteps sounded in the street outside, heavy wooden clogs clacking on the paving stones. The meeting at the ancestral hall was over.

The next morning we learned the details. The meeting had definitely concerned us. The young men were keen on getting that foreign devil and her companion out of the village. Use force if necessary—go to the house where they were staying—destroy the things they'd brought with them—turn them out into the night and let them find some other place to tell about their Jesus. But one of the leading elders hadn't come to the meeting. Without his consent, the younger element didn't dare carry out their drastic threats. Someone was sent to his house with an urgent call to come at once.

When he arrived, his first question was, "What did you call me for?" They told him of these people who had come and were filling their village with talk about Jesus, adding that they were for driving them out.

"Oh!" he said. "So that's it! I thought you wanted to do something constructive, like building up the walls of the village or repairing the gates. As for these people, they are only women; they can't do us any harm. They have come and they will go. Let them alone." And with a few more discouraging words, he dismissed the assembly. We were unmolested.

In Kong Moon we dropped in to see some Baptist missionaries, thinking they would be able to help us find a Bible woman suitable for Saam Tsuen—someone old enough not to be frightened or discouraged by opposition and someone who spoke the dialect. They were very cooperative, saying they would keep it in mind and pray about it.

The Lord provided a Bible woman for us, a middle-aged woman with a kindly face. What she lacked in initiative she made up in stick-to-itiveness. She was unobtrusive in manner, yet had a love for the Lord and for telling about Him to women who had never heard. I went with her to the village to introduce her to Mrs. Lee, the midwife, and to get her started in her work.

After that I went to Saam Tsuen for a few days every two or three months, whenever it was possible to get away from the work in Koon Shan and the outstations. On one of these visits, my attention was called to a little beggar boy, Ah Uen. His parents were dead; he had no brothers or sisters; his nearest relatives were too poor to support him, but they did unite to give two dollars a month to an old beggar woman to take care of him. But the relatives had come to the conclusion that they really ought to do something better for him than that. So when I was there, they asked me if I would take him and let him have an education. I was glad to be able to cooperate, for hadn't K. S. Lee said he would be responsible for any orphans found in his village? When it actually came to their giving the child over to me, they asked me to sign a paper stating that I was only taking him temporarily. He would always be a member of the Lei clan of Saam Tsuen.

The little fellow (about five years old) with his sallow face and soulful eyes looked me full in the face. I told him he might call me "Ah Ma" (as all the children in the orphanage called me). His thin little lips formed the words and then he cuddled up to me as though he had found his long-lost mother. We took him to Mrs. Lee's house where we were staying, gave him a bath, and got him into some clean clothes. The next two nights he shared my bed.

As we were leaving the village two days later, a kindly woman gave him a copper penny which he promptly put in the pocket of his little jacket. When we got to the city of Kong Moon and were walking along the waterfront on our way to get our boat for home, I was carrying my satchel in one hand and had Ah Uen by the other hand. I was watching traffic (only pedestrians and heavily loaded coolies, but plenty of them) when I felt a tugging at my hand. I looked down. Ah Uen was looking up at me imploringly.

An older beggar boy was walking beside us with his hand held out, asking for help. Ah Uen put his hand in his pocket, pulled out his one penny, and gave it to the boy with a smile. He knew what it was to be in need. His gift meant he had faith to believe that from now on his needs would be supplied. He had come into God's family.

About a year later, on a subsequent visit to Saam Tsuen, I took Ah Uen with me. The women of the village were delighted to see him looking so well. He had been completely de-wormed and his sallow complexion had given place to a healthy glow. Even the men noticed him with interest. The intense anti-foreign and anti-Christian attitude was beginning to thaw.

In the meantime the Lord brought Pastor Lei Hok Kei to work with us. He was a middle-aged man with a pleasant face and kind smile. He wasn't an outstanding platform speaker; his strong point was personal evangelism. Mr. Lei Sing Shau, the former opium addict, was now our right-hand man. His Bible studies and messages from the pulpit were used by the Holy Spirit to bless the Christians in Koon Shan and the outstations. What a power for God these two men could be, working together, the gifts of the one complementing those of the other. But as we prayed daily for the work in Saam Tsuen as well as for the work of the Koon Shan area, the Lord seemed to say, "Let Pastor Lei Hok Kei go to Saam Tsuen."

"But we need him here, Lord," I remonstrated.

"Let him go" came the reply.

"But he is our only ordained man and he works so well with Lei Sing Shau," I argued.

"He is of the Lei [Lee] clan and can speak the dialect of Saam Tsuen. Let him go." And of course the Lord won out.

Pastor Lei found a place to stay at the church in Wong Chung, the nearest village to Saam Tsuen. Day after day he walked the distance between the villages to join little groups of men resting under the shade of a tree or at the village gates.

At first his friendly greeting and smile were received at only a small part of their face value. He was a stranger, a man. What could he be wanting by coming to their village? The first question they asked was what his surname was. When they found that he also was a Lei, a long discussion followed about the origin of his branch of the Lei family. In the end it was decided that they had common ancestry. They were brothers; he was no longer a "stranger."

Pastor Lei let it be known that he would like to rent an empty shop in Saam Tsuen's tiny marketplace where he could live and have a place to converse with the "brothers" when they came to see him, instead of just being out under the trees. Finally a young man came to him privately and told him that he had a shop, but the rent would be quite high. Would he be interested? Knowing that K. S. Lee in Shanghai was willing to pay almost any price to get an opening for preaching the Gospel in the village, he consented to look at it. It seems that at the beginning of the year the young man had paid down a whole year's rent on the shop, expecting to use it for a gambling place. But the government had passed strict laws forbidding gambling, and the shop had stood empty since the first of the year. The man very much wanted to get his money back, so if the pastor would pay him the whole year's rent, he could have it. The bargain was made. The place was cleaned up, the walls whitewashed. Benches were made in Kong Moon and brought in by riverboat. Then a sign board "Fook Yam Tong" (Gospel Hall) was put up over the front door. Only then did some of the village elders realize that the preaching of the Gospel had really come in among them. Some were very angry.

One morning an elderly man came into the Gospel Hall. Shaking his fist in the pastor's face, he said, "You have come here to look for rams." ("Ram" was the term used by robbers to indicate the persons whom they had kidnapped. This man was thus accusing the pastor of being an agent for the government to spy on them.)

The pastor wasn't in the least disturbed, but with his usual genial smile called the man "Brother" and asked him to sit down and have a cup of tea, which he was pouring while he talked.

"Rams?" he said. "No, I don't know anything about those. I have come here to look for lost 'lambs' to save them."

The man, not familiar with the Gospel story, missed the significance of the reference to lambs, but somehow seemed to find himself being defeated by the pastor's kind attitude. Once more he turned on him with a shake of his fist, saying, "You get out of here!" Then he walked out of the building, never to come back to make trouble.

Mr. Lei spoke every night in the little Gospel Hall and in the daytime several men always dropped in to have a talk with him. Over a cup of tea they asked questions about how this Gospel could apply to their own needs. Among those who became earnest inquirers was a young man who in the end confessed that he was among those who hadn't wanted me and my companion to talk to the women of the village about the Lord Jesus when we had first gone there.

On one of my trips to Saam Tsuen, my attention was called to a boy of about eight or ten. His father was dead and his mother was ill. With the consent of the village authorities, we took him to Koon Shan to go to school. On the way we also took his sick mother to the Presbyterian hospital in Kong Moon. The boy's given name was Chan To, which meant Pearl-peach. After he had been in school for two or three years and become a Christian, he changed the characters for his name to others with the same sound but which meant True-disciple. Later when he was in

Chung Hing Bible Institute, he found that the Mandarin pronunciation of his name was so similar to the English word "gentle" that he took "Gentle" for his English name. Today, Gentle Lee is the pastor of Hebron Church in Kowloon, Hong Kong. God had His purpose in leading us to Saam Tsuen.

CHAPTER FOURTEEN

The Lord Pays the Bills

* * *

The contact with K. S. Lee had brought us this new fellowship in the work in Saam Tsuen and it had also brought us financial help during that time of "depression." Almost every time he sent money for the work in his village, he included a gift for Hebron as well. We never knew when these gifts were coming, but they often came opportunely.

One time when I was working on the list of payments to be made on the first of the month, there just didn't seem to be enough money to go around. Our workers had received only 80 or 90 percent of their allowances for the last two months. I felt strongly that I ought to give them the full amount this month, but then that wouldn't leave enough for the rice bill (usually about $100 monthly).

I sent up a silent prayer, "Father, what shall I do?"

"Let the workers have theirs" came the reassuring answer. The next day when the workers were gratefully receiving their full allowances, the postman came with a letter from K. S. Lee. It enclosed a check for the work in Saam Tsuen and an extra $200 for the work of Hebron. The rice bill was paid in full with some to spare.

By the 1930s our industrial department was not only paying for itself but even brought in a small profit (much appreciated in those days when money was short). We were making silk quilts in addition to the weaving and lace-making with which we had started several years previous-ly. The filling of these quilts was pure silk "wool," made from processed waste silk cocoons, the cocoons from which the moths had hatched so that they were not usable for making into silk thread. The quilts were lightweight and very warm—perfect for the cold winter nights.

We sold them first to personal friends in Canton. They told their friends about them and the demand increased. We took a sample quilt to the big Sincere Department Store in Canton; they gave us a trial order. The quilts sold so fast that they then gave us one order after another. We also made mosquito netting, weaving the material by the yard and then making it up into bed nets for several of the big mission hospitals.

This industrial activity employed quite a number of girls and women. Even the old women in our home for aged widows worked on the cocoons for the quilts since it was such light work and required no special skill; they were all so happy to be employed.

By now, we needed someone to look after the orders to see that they were filled promptly and the goods deliv-ered. Po Tak, the boy with whom we began the orphanage back in 1919, was now a teenager. He had finished primary school and then had two years in a technical school. Now he wanted to be our "right-hand helper" and he fitted in beautifully, relieving me of a lot of detail work.

About this time Nam Hoi County, in which we were located, decided to put on a county fair. It was the first of its kind and was an example of the way in which govern-ment activities, even down to the county level, were becoming modernized under Chiang Kai-Shek's leadership. The authorities asked us to give an exhibit of our silk quilts at the fair. We prepared a glass-topped box with samples showing the steps in processing the waste cocoons and then showed a completed silk quilt. Imagine our surprise when we were awarded first prize! The reason for awarding us the prize was that we had produced a "thing of beauty and usefulness from a waste product." It was typical of what our Lord was doing in human hearts all around us.

One bright morning in October 1934, I woke up with the realization that certain financial obligations had to be met that day. I committed them to the Lord in my early devotions, but even after breakfast the burden for them was still on my heart. The German sisters and some of the Bible students were going to Tai Tung for evangelistic work; didn't I want to go with them? Yes, I would like to go, but I felt strongly that I must stay at home and see to this financial matter.

After the others had gone, I checked over my books. There were no accounts receivable. There was nothing in the bank on which I could draw (there was Saam Tsuen money there, but it was not for Hebron). There was nothing in the cash drawer. I talked with the Lord about it and He reminded me of the words of Habakkuk: "Although the fig tree shall not blossom, neither shall fruit be in the vines; the labour of the olive shall fail, and the fields shall yield no meat; the flock shall be cut off from the fold, and there shall be no herd in the stalls: yet I will rejoice in the Lord, I will joy in the God of my salvation." I did rejoice in Him, knowing that He had a way. The burden was lifted from my heart and I went about my routine office work.

A little over an hour later, I heard a voice calling me at the front door. There stood one of our Christian women from a village a few miles away. I invited her in and we sat and visited. She asked if I remembered that four years ago she had gone to the hospital in Canton at my recommendation. At that time she wasn't well and was unable to work (as a silk weaver). She then reminded me that I had paid her hospital bill, which she had appreciated very much and was only sorry that she hadn't repaid it before. Did I remember how much it was? No, I'd completely forgotten. She knew the year and month and told me to look it up in my account book, so I did. The amount was $40.

"I have come to pay that old bill," she said, and from her little market basket she brought out four $10 rolls of silver coin. It seemed as though it came from the Lord's own hand. I told her how a certain amount, less than $40, was needed very much that day. I simply didn't have it, but had trusted that the Lord would bring it to me in some way. She had been His messenger.

During this time of financial shortage we received word that quite a substantial amount had been left to us in the will of a certain lady in Santa Barbara. I knew very little about her other than that she was a member of a well-to-do Catholic family who had made their money in the liquor business. She was a good customer in our store and every time she came in she asked, "What word is there from the daughter in China?" Mother frequently gave her my letters to read. God evidently used them to touch her heart, for when she made out her will, she included "Mrs. Hitchcock's daughter in China." When we heard of the bequest, we wished that the money would hurry up and come while it was still worth something. The exchange rate was becoming worse every month. Sometimes we lost as much as $200 or $300 a month on just the rate of exchange.

Twice a year one large payment caused us concern: the expenses for our older boys going away to high school. There were fees for tuition, board, dormitory, and books as well as a little something for incidentals. The school authorities in the Wesleyan Mission High School at Fat Shan were kind. They told us we needn't worry about paying the fees at the opening of the school term; we could take our time and pay when convenient. Being confident that the money from the lady's will would be coming eventually, we sent the boys back to school at the beginning of the term. Month after month went by with the bill still unpaid, but during those months the rate of exchange began to improve. Week by week there was a change for the better. Finally at the end of the year, the money came when there was such a good rate that we had enough to meet the expenses for the boys and many other obligations with some left over. The Lord had timed it in His own way.

Sister Marie Luise had been chosen to work with the group for special meetings in the outstations during the spring. That fully occupied her time. The Door of Hope, a rescue home for former slave girls, wrote us urgently, asking that Sister Margarete come to Canton to take charge of the work while the director was home on furlough. We didn't see how we could spare her from the work in Koon Shan, but at last we compromised, letting her go for a few months until the Door of Hope could find someone else.

At the same time there was a little upset among the teachers in the primary school. There was no one to teach fifth and sixth grade arithmetic and English. Thinking that it would give me good contact with the schoolchildren, many of whom were from heathen homes, I volunteered for the position. In a way I enjoyed it, but it was confining. By the time summer vacation came, I was having other thoughts about it. As I wrote home to Mother:

> Saturday morning I had a nice quiet time reading my Bible and also read some from Hudson Taylor. I have come to realize that my staying tied up here in Koon Shan this last half year has not been the best thing. I didn't come to China to teach school and I don't think that it has been altogether pleasing to the Lord that I did this spring. I had to neglect my office work and

also the outstation visiting, and neither of these
ought to have been neglected. Well, we learn by
experience, and I do pray that the Lord will guide me
clearly step by step that I may not make mistakes in
the future. I have given myself to accounts yesterday
and today and got more accomplished in these two
days than I had done in that line all this half year. I
will try not to get so far behind again.

CHAPTER FIFTEEN

The War Begins

* * *

In September of 1936 the political situation in our part of the country began to change for the better. The corrupt provincial governor absconded, turning his authority over to the central government. That gave Chiang Kai-shek control of Kwong Tung Province and immediately his "New Life" program was put into operation. One aspect of this closed down all gambling and opium dens. (Even "ma chong" and bridge played in private homes were under the ban.) Attractive posters everywhere reminded people to be respectful to the elderly, courteous to everyone, prompt in keeping appointments, and upright in business. People became conscious of the fact that their country was worth their patriotism.

The big event of the year was just after the first of October when my niece Margaret came to help me for a while. I went to Hong Kong to meet her ship, but because of my tight schedule, we had no time to stay with friends in Hong Kong. I whisked Margaret, or "Peggy" as we came to call her, away by the afternoon train to Canton and then by the night boat on to Koon Shan. It was a sudden change to things entirely Chinese, but she was game for it.

The day we arrived in Koon Shan there was a baptismal service and a lot of the Christians were in from the out-stations for the Lord's Supper—and also to see the "new missionary." The next day I was due in one of the out-stations for two days of special meetings. The only thing to do was to take Peggy with me, for she as yet knew only the simplest Chinese words and no one in Koon Shan spoke English. By taking a little bread and jam along as an extra snack, she got along fine with the Chinese meals.

After two or three days at home allowing me to teach my classes in our Bible school and giving Peggy a little start on the office work, I was off to another outstation for two more days. When we went on trips involving boat travel, Peggy took along her notebook and I dictated letters, which she typed when we got back home.

In February the two sisters came back from their furlough in Germany. Peggy got time for more systematic language study and with someone to help with the children and Bible school as well as outstation work, I found my load lightening a bit. My mind and heart went out to places still without a regular Christian witness. In talking with our Chinese workers about this, I found that both Mr. Cheung and the Bible woman were keen on making another trip to Pak Nai, a place we had found open to the Gospel on a previous trip. We decided to go there during Easter vacation and take a boy from the Bible school.

We left Koon Shan before daylight on the morning of April 5th and arrived at Pak Nai about three o'clock in the afternoon. The last part of the way the paths were nothing but deep mud, for it had been raining nearly ten days. We found lodging in a small inn that left much to be desired in the way of cleanliness, but otherwise wasn't at all bad (ten cents a night included room, bed, bedbugs, and kitchen privileges). The days passed quickly in visiting the neighboring villages, preaching in the market, and getting into personal contact with those who lived near us.

We had taken 160 gospel portions with us and 870 tracts, which was not enough to supply the demand. We estimated that we could easily have sold another 150 or 200 gospels.

We were happy with the opportunities to give out the Word of God, sorry we hadn't taken more gospels and tracts with us, and disappointed that we hadn't found a place where a Christian worker could live and be a continual witness for the Lord in that area. But we were confident that we had gone in response to the Lord's leading and we could trust Him for further guidance in the future.

In June K. S. Lee came from Shanghai with a friend to visit Saam Tsuen, his home village. It was interesting to see his enthusiasm as he recognized landmarks he hadn't seen for 30 years or more. But it was best of all to hear his ringing testimony for the Lord as he spoke to one after another of the villagers. They were all his people—uncles, brothers, cousins—and he was not ashamed to let them know that he belonged 100 percent to Jesus Christ. He was pleased to see the high respect the people had for Pastor Lei Hok Kei and to see the attitude of open friendliness to the Gospel on the part of men and women alike. He felt that the next step was to find a trained nurse and open a free clinic especially for the children. (Infected scratches, sores, and boils were common during the summer in the fly-infested village.)

In July I was in our outstation Kat Lei for a few days of special meetings. One day the two men of our party went to a teahouse in the market for a noonday snack. When they came back to the house, they had a newspaper with them. I saw them both reading it at the same time, one looking over the shoulder of the other with concern on their faces.

"What's interesting in today's news?" I asked them.

"There's been a clash between the Japanese military and our Chinese soldiers just outside of Tientsin. We don't know what it may lead to," they replied.

That clash was the beginning of the Sino-Japanese war, and eight years of hardship and suffering followed for thousands of China's peasants.

K. S. Lee, with quick foresight, moved his family to Hong Kong just before Shanghai was bombed. Not long afterward Canton was also bombed, and several government schools were moved from the city. An agricultural school specializing in sericulture came to Koon Shan. A teacher-training school for girls came to one of the villages west of us. A few of the students or teachers in these schools were Christians and came to the church on Sunday, and through them we had contacts with other students. Eventually we started Bible study classes for them on Saturday afternoons.

Patriotism was running high. Everybody wanted to do something to help. In North China thousands were already homeless and destitute. The suggestion was made that if those who still had home and food wanted to help, they could go without one meal a week and send that money to the needy. The Chinese of our area ate only two meals a day, one about half past nine in the morning and the other at five in the afternoon; both consisted of rice with fish (or meat) and vegetables. To go without one meal was to cut off half a day's rations. Many Christians gladly offered to help in this way.

The children in the orphanage heard of it and wanted to have a share. Sunday morning was the meal that was to be given up, but we insisted that it was to be entirely voluntary. Saturday evening I was handed a sheet of paper on which were the names of the 25 who wanted to go without their Sunday morning meal; 22 were children; the others were the women who took care of them. When I went to the prayer room that morning, several pairs of kek (wooden shoes) were at the door. Inside were little

114

boys kneeling and praying for their country and for those suffering in the war. I had been made treasurer of this project and by the first of January I had about $160 to turn in to the relief headquarters in Canton.

Bombing became more frequent in Canton and in other cities of our province. Traveling became more hazardous as highways and railroads were bombed. But in spite of the dangers, our workers and I planned another trip to Pak Nai for the Easter vacation week. Some advised against our going, but we felt that the Lord had said "Go," so we went. After our arrival in the town, Mr. Cheung and I went to visit the village elder to establish our identity as Christian workers, lest we be under suspicion as Japanese spies. He was very friendly, so we presented him with a gospel and told him of the wonderful saving power of the Lord Jesus.

During the few days there we again contacted an elderly woman who on our previous visit had accepted the Lord as her Savior. We found her wholeheartedly trusting in Jesus to the extent of her understanding, having done away with all idol worship. We spoke to crowds in the market and in the villages, sold all the gospels we had brought, and gave out all the tracts. We had many personal contacts and found receptive hearts. A few months later that town was bombed and destroyed. That was our last opportunity to go there with the Gospel.

CHAPTER SIXTEEN

The Children's Refuge Is Born

* * *

My parents were going to have their golden wedding anniversary in August 1938 and they wanted both Peggy and me to be at home for that occasion. We were able to book passage on a ship sailing from Hong Kong the latter part of June. But there were so many things to be done before leaving: another trip to Saam Tsuen, Bible school examinations and graduation, and final meetings with the girls in the schools that had evacuated to Koon Shan from Canton. (Thirty-two years later I was riding on a crowded train in Hong Kong, by then a city of nearly five million, when a Chinese woman approached me with a smile. Something about her seemed to bring back a memory. Where had I seen her? She courteously asked me if possibly I was the missionary who had formerly lived in Koon Shan. When I replied in the affirmative, she went on to say that she was one of the girls in the teacher-training school and had attended the Bible classes. She told how much the Christian fellowship meant to her and many others. She was now a teacher in a school in Hong Kong.)

K. S. Lee and his wife and youngest son were on the same ship with us (but not in the same class), on their first leg of a journey around the world. Later that summer we had them as guests in our home in Santa Barbara.

My parents had been in business for 50 years and had

117

many friends in all walks of life. The celebration was held right in the store, it being so much more central and accessible than our residence. Counters and fixtures were moved to provide space. We got a big rug and set up a tea table. The pastors of almost every church in town were guests and even the city mayor dropped in.

In October that year Canton fell to the Japanese with much loss of life and destruction of property. The first week of December the enemy took over Koon Shan. Because of the heavy bombing previously, the local Chinese officials had withdrawn across the West River. When the Japanese army officers came to the mission property and saw the two German sisters there, they were pleased. Wasn't Germany confederate with Japan? They wanted the two Germans to exult with them in their victory both in Canton and now in Koon Shan. But our sisters hardly knew how to answer them. Their hearts were loyal to China and they hated to see the people suffering. It was probably just as well that I was in the homeland at the time, for the invaders' first impression of the Koon Shan Mission was "good."

I longed to be back. My father was then 83 years old and it was hard for him to give his approval for his "little girl" to go to a war area with all its unknown dangers. The matter was taken daily to the Lord in prayer, for we all realized that war or no war, the safest place to be was in God's will. Reassuring letters came from the field. By the middle of February 1939 I was ready to set out across the Pacific once more with the unanimous approval and wholehearted prayer support of the Hebron Home Board. My father and I realized that we wouldn't see each other again this side of Heaven, but the confidence that we would meet there brought us joy in spite of the moisture in our eyes.

One morning on board ship I was sitting alone on deck

with my Bible. I had come to Psalm 115 in my daily reading and was wandering slowly down the page through the verses. Suddenly the words of the 14th verse seemed to stand right out from the page: "The Lord shall increase you more and more, you and your children." Something about that "you" was so personal. And then "children." Yes, we had carried on work among children in Koon Shan for about 20 years, but most of all our hearts yearned for spiritual children. Here was the promise of increase. I appropriated the promise and went forward expectantly.

Sister Margarete and other friends met me in Hong Kong. They acquainted me with the new means of travel and briefed me on what to expect back in Koon Shan. No commercial boats were running between Hong Kong and Canton. That part of the trip had to be made by British gunboat, which necessitated my leaving a good part of my baggage with friends in Hong Kong. Canton, of course, was in Japanese hands. Large parts of the city were in ruins. Lawlessness and disorder prevailed. Conditions in the country districts were worse. The Japanese had driven out the Chinese authorities but were hardly attempting to establish any government themselves.

Almost no boats traveled the rivers, for banditry was prevalent. At last we found one that would take us within three or four miles of Koon Shan; we would have to walk the rest of the way. This caused us to leave practically all the remaining baggage with friends in Canton, taking with us only what we would be able to carry ourselves when walking. It was all of the Lord's arranging and He gave us a safe journey.

Mr. Lei Sing Shau, our Chinese assistant in the work, had been earnestly praying that there would be no conspicuous homecoming with a large display of baggage, for he realized the danger to which we would expose ourselves under the present lawlessness. To walk quietly into the old streets unannounced and not met, with only a small satchel apiece, was the wisest way to arrive.

How the town had changed during those few months! Only a few buildings remained along the waterfront and a few more along the upper street at the foot of the mountain. The center of the town was in ruins, blank walls towering above tumbled piles of broken bricks and tiles. The mission property was still intact, however. The church building had been struck by one or two small bombs, wrecking the roof and most of the third floor, but the strong brick walls were undamaged. Later a provisional roof was put on, which made the auditorium usable and protected the building from further deterioration. Having walked up through the ruins of the town, how pleasant it was to walk into our "Shun Kwong Uen," the Garden of Sterling Light. Everything was just the same: the happy faces of our children, our workers and colleagues, the flowers, trees, buildings, all the gift of God's love to us and the object of His tender care and keeping.

Although the condition of the town was bad, the condition of the people was worse. There was no government, no law, no court of appeal. Anyone could do anything he wanted, provided he had a faster gun than the other fellow. Transportation was tied up. Industry was at a standstill with no market for silk, the principal product of the Sai Chiu District. Food prices were rising daily. There was no security whatever for life, limb, or property. The small earnings of thousands of people were rapidly being exhausted by high prices or were being taken by any man with a gun. We longed to help the suffering people, but what could we do in the face of such great need?

One day in April, Mr. Lei came back from the teahouse with a suggestion. (In South China the teahouse is where the men congregate at noon or in the evening for tea and a snack to hear the latest news and gossip.) He suggested that we open a refuge for the starving children. Day after day at the teahouse he had listened to tales of families who had fled from Canton at the time of the Japanese occupation, thinking that conditions would be better in their rural village. But conditions kept getting worse, and their meager savings were being used up. They were starving themselves trying to keep their children alive. If we could take their children temporarily, the parents could go elsewhere, find employment, and eventually take back their children. Perhaps we could take in 50 or a 100 children for a few months until the rice harvest when the situation might be somewhat relieved.

Was this God's plan for us? Was this what He meant when on board ship He had given the verse saying He would "increase you more and more, you and your children"? We laid it before the Lord in prayer and He gave us great freedom and peace of mind that it was the thing to do.

Through the medium of the teahouse, Mr. Lei let it become known to the village elders what we had in mind and they at once expressed themselves heartily in favor. The principal of the government school adjoining the mission property offered his school buildings for the use of the children's refuge. Nothing could have suited our purpose better. God was providing what we would need.

The problem was how to secure cash in hand for work of this sort. The mission might have plenty of money in the bank in Canton or Hong Kong, but getting it out to Koon Shan over 30 miles of roads or rivers where robbers were ready to meet one at every turn—that was the difficulty. But we were confident that if this work was God's plan, He would find a way.

We were still making plans and cleaning school buildings when the wife of a Chinese doctor who had lived in

Koon Shan for over 20 years came to my office one morning and asked for a private interview. In a whisper she told me that they could no longer stay. Evil men were planning to rob and kidnap them. They must leave and go to Hong Kong. But they couldn't take their savings with them, for they would be robbed on the way. Could she leave her money with me and could I give her a check which she could get cashed in Hong Kong? What a look of relief came over her face when I assured her that I could.

She left the house and returned half an hour later carrying a bundle of bamboo sticks. Standing behind a door where she felt safely out of sight from all windows, she began drawing little rolls of bills from the inside of the hollow bamboo. Soon she gave me an amount equivalent to 200 American dollars and I gave her a check written in English which no robber would ever suspect was money. The precious bills were placed in a tin can and buried in the garden for the time when they would be needed for the children. It seemed another token from God that He would supply for the new work He wanted us to do.

One afternoon a few days later, while the cleaning was still going on in the school buildings, I was called to the door by the loud voice of the woman who carried water for the few shops in the market.

"Here's a little girl for you," she said as she let slide from her back a child who was more like a skeleton than any living person I had ever seen. Her eyes were sunk deep in her head, her neck was so tiny it seemed your fingers could close around it, her arms and legs were pipestems. She was too weak to stand.

"You'll take her, won't you?" the woman went on. "The men in the shops told me to carry her here, and you would take her."

The child had been a servant girl in a village not far

from Koon Shan. Her starving owners had told her to go out and shift for herself. She had dragged her weary feet along the dike to Koon Shan, hoping to beg from the few shops left in the market. After two nights in the street, she had stumbled over some broken bricks and was too weak and exhausted to get up. The men in the shops, knowing of the mission's plan to open a refuge for starving children, had given the water-carrier a few coppers and told her to bring the child to us.

"Yes, we'll take her," I said as I looked spellbound into those deep, sad eyes. Thin rice soup was all we dared give her that night, for she'd been without food too long to have a good meal at the start. But Tung Kuk, for that was her name, began to pick up right away and within a week she was a different girl. At the end of a month, her face was as round as the full moon. Later she became a helper among the younger children in the refuge.

CHAPTER SEVENTEEN

Bandits—Great and Small

* * *

A few days later the afternoon session of our monthly day of prayer was just coming to a close when shots suddenly rang out. Not just a few stray shots, but continuous firing that kept on hour after hour. At first we didn't know the cause. Could the Japanese be coming again? But why should they fire on the town when it was already, theoretically, in their hands?

Finally, in spite of bullets whizzing through our garden, some braver ones climbed to a lookout post on our tallest building. From there they saw that the town was practically surrounded by robbers, probably a thousand of them. They wanted to terrorize the few people left in the town so that no one would resist when they came in at dark to take whatever they could find. It had been commonly reported in robber circles (and word had been brought to us) that not much was worth robbing in Koon Shan except two pawnshops and the missionaries' residence.

In South China the pawnshops were towerlike buildings, six or eight stories high, owned by the town bankers. Well-to-do people would put their fur-lined winter clothing into the pawnshop at the beginning of summer for safekeeping and good care. There was sure to be plenty of loot if they could open the heavy iron doors. Were we also to fall into the hands of these merciless men?

Earlier in the day the mail had brought a letter from home, but because of the meetings and the many people who had come to see me, I'd had no time to read it. Now there was time. My parents had learned from a letter written them by the German sisters before my return that our Chinese friends had warned them of the great danger from the breakdown of local government. With the threat of banditry, we might lose everything. My parents went straight to their knees and poured out their hearts to God, asking Him to keep His protecting hand over His children there on the mission field. They were confident that their prayer was heard, and now the letter of assurance came from them just when the bandits were at our doors. I went to the little groups of women and children huddled in the dugout and in the corners of the dining room and told them I had word from America that God would protect us in just this sort of situation.

The gunfire kept up far into the night, pawnshops and houses were looted, fires were started. Still the dugout was left early, supper cooked and eaten, and an atmosphere of quiet trust pervaded the mission premises. It seemed that the presence of God Himself had come down and was watching over all.

At about half past ten, signal shots were fired; then came quiet; the "big" robbers had gone. But soon shouts and angry voices from a distance let us know that the "little" men, the rabble, were at work taking things that the "big" men had left.

We greeted one another with radiant faces the next morning in the Garden of Sterling Light. To have passed through such a night and still be untouched was a miracle. But the reign of terror had only begun. Efforts at keeping order in the town were now entirely abandoned and many of those who had formerly been employed as police turned to robbing. Night after night, hundreds of armed men broke into house after house and looted at will. The orphanage, which was temporarily occupying the house under the banyans to the west of "Sterling Light," was broken into four nights and anywhere from four to ten times a night by different bands of men. Mosquito nets, bedding, clothing, and even the thermos bottles for the babies' night food were taken. But each morning Kwai Ling, Yan Tin, and their helpers had smiles of praise to God that they had been spared personal harm and that some things were still left. These wicked men did not even spare the old women's home, which occupied the former industrial buildings. The poor, patient old women were forced out of bed night after night at gunpoint to be searched and then rudely treated when no money was forthcoming.

The fifth night, the 14th of May, a sound of splintering wood at midnight brought us all wide awake. The robbers were in the playground next door. Then there was a few shots and shouts and the sound of tumbling bricks. They had broken over the garden wall! Mr. Lei met them at the break in the wall, saying "Don't shoot! Give me a man to talk to me, I have something to tell you!"

"What do you want to say?" asked a gruff voice, as the point of a gun was stuck into his ribs.

Mr. Lei then explained that not much was worth their while in the various buildings. The things of most value to them would be found in his house, the last one at the upper end of the path. They might take anything from his house that they wanted on one condition, that they take nothing from the house of the missionaries.

"These foreigners have come here to help us," he explained. "They are opening a refuge for starving children; just tomorrow morning they begin to receive the children. Now, if you rob them of their things, it is the same as driving them away. They cannot stay on here and work without their clothing, bedding, utensils, and such things. If you drive them away, who will save the destitute children of this whole district? Probably there will be children of your own village who will starve to death and there will be no one to save them. Now, if you will promise not to touch their things, you can go and help yourselves to what you want from my house."

"We promise! We promise!" came from the group of 12 or 15 rough-looking men who had listened quietly while Mr. Lei spoke. In another moment they were rushing up the path to his house, while the leader kept hold of Mr. Lei's hand and listened to all he had to say about not breaking locks or molesting the medicine chest which they wouldn't understand. Surely God had touched the heart of that robber chieftain so that he restrained his men.

After about two hours, he said to Mr. Lei, "I must go and ask the foreigners for some money."

Knowing that it couldn't be avoided, Mr. Lei consented. "But," he added, "remember you are to take nothing from their house."

They came up our steps—those midnight callers—the leader and three of his men. Sister Margarete and I opened the door and invited them in, guns and all. The chieftain, in a kindly voice, told me he had heard that we had had $4,000 sent to us. He wanted to ask for the loan of half of it. That was such an absurdly large amount for those days that we laughed in spite of ourselves and then told him a little something of how mission money is contributed, the nickels, dimes, and quarters from children's savings and the sacrificial gifts from hard-working people. He seemed perplexed.

"Well, little or much, let us have something," he said at last.

I opened our money drawer and one of the men scooped the contents into his hands. That drawer had been prepared night after night for just such a visit. Not much was in it and some of the bills weren't in current use, but it was enough so that they didn't demand more. Our consciences weren't troubled that we said nothing about that precious packet buried in the garden, or the little rolls tucked in the bamboo lattice of the porch or certain tin boxes hidden in drainpipes. The men toured the house, but true to their promise they took none of our things.

Just as they were about to leave, someone said, "Search their persons!" At once rough hands and pistol points fumbled at Sister Margarete's and my clothing while Mr. Lei remonstrated, "Don't carry it too far!"

"I have my key and my watch," I replied as I took them from my pocket and held them in my open hand. The watch passed quickly to eager hands to be scrutinized under the light of several flashlights, while I explained, "You see it's only silver and it has my name engraved on the back. Wherever you take it, people will know it belongs to me."

"Give it back to her," the leader said, and the faithful little old timepiece again occupied my pocket.

At about two o'clock they were ready to leave and assembled their sacks of booty from Mr. Lei's house. But another danger presented itself: almost 200 lesser robbers had gathered outside our walls, just waiting for these "big" men to leave so that they could come and strip the place of everything. Mr. Lei keenly realized the danger and appealed to the chieftain, "You have understood the situation; you have given us 'face' [that is, respected us. Opposite: 'to lose face']. You know that there's no reasoning with these lesser men. Now it's your responsibility to see to it that we are kept safe until daylight."

"Don't worry about that," the chieftain replied. And then as he and his men went out through the gate that Mr. Lei opened for them, he turned and apologized for what had taken place. Those who had been lurking outside the walls gradually melted away. All was quiet.

Morning came and again we rejoiced. "The angel of the Lord encampeth round about them that fear him and delivereth them." The house of one of our neighbors had been broken into about two nights previously. First the "big" men and then the rabble had taken all that they wanted. For 15 hours things were being taken out of that house and when they were through, nothing was left but trash. Our house would have been the same had it not been for God's power to touch the heart of a robber chieftain. Mr. Lei was happier than he had been for months. The experience had caused him the loss of material things but had brought him spiritual gain.

But there was no time to waste that morning. As had been planned, Sister Margarete was to take five babies from the orphanage to a foundling home in Canton. With quilts, nets, thermos bottles gone, and with robbers breaking in nearly every night, the care of the little ones had become very difficult. Two Chinese women went along to help care for them on the way. They had gone scarcely two miles when their little boat was abruptly boarded by a man with a gun who roughly ordered Sister Margarete ashore, saying, "You have eaten bread long enough; now we will let you eat bran for a while." "Bran" was the term applied to the food given to those who were kidnapped by bandits. So it was his intention to kidnap the little group!

"Oh, no! That cannot be!" cried the younger of the two Chinese women. "She does not eat bread [considered a luxury]; she eats rice soup along with the rest of us."

Even Sister Margarete's brave heart seemed ready to fail at the thought of being kidnapped. Tears came to her eyes while tears were already coursing down the cheeks of the two Chinese women. Just then the babies all began to cry. Such an onslaught of feminine tears was too much

130

even for the man with the gun.

"Go along then," he said and pointed across the fields.

"But we don't know the way to walk from here and how can we carry the babies?" protested the Chinese woman.

"Back to the boat then," he said somewhat impatiently.

Seated in the boat again, tears were dried and praise given to God who had delivered them from the hands of another wicked man.

In the meantime, back in Koon Shan we were having further evidences of God's loving care. After breakfast the money which had been placed elsewhere the previous night had just been brought back but not yet put away when Mr. Lei walked past the door and remarked, "Robbers are here again. They will be in the gate in another minute."

I grabbed the precious packet of bills and rushed upstairs to conceal them in a secret crevice. Stepping out onto the upstairs porch, I was visible to the armed men in the school playground next door. One of them, with canny premonition, called out, "There, she is hiding her money now!"

I recoiled into the house, quickly put the packet into a second-best secret place, and was at the door to meet the men as they came up the path. They were a formidable-looking party, armed with various types of guns and even hand grenades. They insisted they were searching only for arms; they claimed to be the town police and said they needed more arms and ammunition. But from the way they searched the house, it was evident they wanted to see what might be left from the raid of the previous night and make plans for getting their share.

As soon as they had gone, Mr. Lei learned that the whole bunch of them were from a village whose "elder" was a good friend of his. Without wasting a moment's time, he went straight to that village and found his friend. This fine, upright man not only expressed regret at what had been done, but at once called the leader who had taken the men to search our house and rebuked him sternly. He then called for a meeting in the ancestral hall of all the older men of his clan. They discussed the situation and decided that their clan should stand back of the mission and its work; they would not allow anyone to molest us. (They stood true to this decision through the remaining years of the war.) That very night they would send two men to watch the mission property. These men were unarmed, but they were elderly men whose word should have weight with the younger ones whose hearts were bent on looting.

After that exhausting day, I was just sitting down to an early supper when someone came to the door with a breathless, "They're coming again!" And there on the terraced graves of the hillside outside the back gate were 50 or more armed men.

The next morning we learned that these men from the mountaintop were in league with the men who had come in the morning. Their intention had been to attack the mission property that night from front and back and simply walk off with everything. But those men on the hillside waited in vain for their accomplices. At dark, the two new watchmen came. Somehow word reached the marauders that village men had been sent to watch the place and they slunk away in the darkness.

CHAPTER EIGHTEEN

Instead of Thy Father Shall Be Thy Children

* * *

T he next day, the 15th of May 1939, the Hebron Children's Refuge became a reality. Little did we realize what it would mean during coming years. It became the means of saving hundreds of little lives and of leading many souls to the Lord Jesus Christ. It also grew to have wide influence all through the Sai Ch'iu District and even into Free China. It determined the direction of the mission's activities during the remaining years of the war.

Within a few days, 50 children arrived. People came with such pitiful tales of hardship and hunger and the children were so thin and emaciated that we couldn't refuse them. Day after day we were besieged with requests to take in another and another. In some cases the parents had been killed in the fighting or had died of hunger or sickness. In other cases the parents were mere skeletons and had nothing more to feed their children; they wanted them kept alive even though they themselves had to die. The number went up to 100, then 150, then 200.

When the children were first received, they were so weak from hunger that they sat in rows like so many wooden dolls. But after about a week of regular feeding they became normal, lively, happy children.

As the number of children increased, we needed more helpers. Many Christians in our outstations had lost all

133

means of earning a living and were facing starvation. We let them come to the Children's Refuge and work for no pay other than enough to eat and the necessities of daily life which were given them from general supplies.

The fact that we could have supplies, or even food, for so large a number of people was nothing less than miraculous. Little was to be had in the makeshift shacks which had replaced the former shops in one short street among the ruins of Koon Shan. Roads and rivers leading to other towns where supplies were available were unsafe for anyone with money in his pocket. But just as the need arose for some way to meet the predicament, a businessman came to us with a proposition. He was known as Po Luk and was a leading member of the village from which the worst of the robbers came. (In fact, he was the "elder" to whom Mr. Lei had appealed just after the robbers had been in our house.) He was a man who liked to do good.

Now he proposed that we let him buy our staples for us: rice, salt, oil, beans, soap, etc. All he asked was that we give him a receipt for value received each time that he delivered any commodities to us. Then after a few months he would ask us to pay the money by check to an address in Macao or Hong Kong where his son would be going to school. Whereas it would have been impossible for us to have gone to other towns to buy supplies, Po Luk's men could come safely with their precious loads, for practically no one in the whole district dared to molest any member of that powerful clan. It even happened one time near the end of the Chinese year, when robbing is always at its worst, that our supply of rice for the next half month (approximately 2,500 pounds) was carried to the door of our Refuge under armed escort. And those armed guards were none other than the robbers of Po Luk's village!

There seemed to be no end to the requests for admittance to the Refuge and with the Lord's help we tried to take in all the really needy cases. By June we had so many babies that we hardly knew how to care for them all. Word came from a foundling home in Hong Kong that they would take eight babies if we could get them there. We prayed about it and it seemed the thing to do, though travel from Koon Shan to Canton was difficult. I walked the first ten miles to a point where I could get a boat for the city. Po Tak went with me so as to be able to go back and give a report on the kind of a trip I had. All went well, the only incident occurring when a Japanese soldier pointed his bayonet at me and told me to "Kow-tow." I nodded my head respectfully and went on my way. Two Chinese women with the eight babies went a roundabout way in a covered rowboat. We met in Canton as arranged, and the next day we went on to Hong Kong by American gunboat.

My trip to Hong Kong at that time was opportune. K. S. Lee and his wife were living there then. I had corresponded with them and Mr. Lee had put part of one of my letters in the daily newspaper. When I arrived, people said, "Oh, I know about the work you are doing." I had never thought of asking for money; I just told stories of bandits, hardship, starving children, and people fairly thrust money into my hands. With K. S. Lee's recommendation, I opened an account in a Hong Kong bank where they could deposit money for our work after I returned to Koon Shan. It was remarkable that I chose this particular bank for later when actual cash was needed in the Refuge, it had some means of delivering fresh new bills to any place in the Japanese-occupied area. Just how they managed it when there were robbers everywhere was more than we could understand, but we got the money. K. S. Lee's friends were generous with their gifts and told us to take in more children. They would see to it that they were fed.

When I got back from that trip to Hong Kong, I received word from home of the death of my dear father: "Absent from the body, but present with the Lord." Psalm 45, with a little different wording, came to my mind: "Instead of thy father shall be thy children, whom thou shalt make princes in all the earth."

A memorial service was held in Koon Shan for him. I wrote home about it:

> The workers and some Christians came from most of the outstations; more would have come except for the fact that there is so much danger of robbers on the way. There were about 300 present at the service; among them were some of our Koon Shan friends who are not even Christians—the men who have proved themselves so friendly and helpful during these troubled times.
>
> Each of the stations and some of the individual Christians presented big silk banners which were hung up all across the front of the meeting room behind the platform. These banners had Chinese characters on them expressing appreciation of Papa's love and faithfulness to the Lord or of his spirit of self-denial in sending the Gospel here to Sai Ch'iu. His picture hung in the background above a cross of flowers; dwarf palm leaves, so arranged that they looked like a big butterfly, a symbol of resurrection, made a background for the picture.
>
> The service lasted nearly two hours; there were songs by the orphanage children, by the kindergarten, and even by the children from the Refuge. Over and over through the service as I looked at dear Papa's picture, I was reminded of the words, "Instead of thy father shall be thy children." It was certainly good of the Chinese Christians to pay such a tribute to Papa's memory. In addition to the silk banners and some sixteen wreaths made from such flowers and greens as they could secure here, they also gave me about $30 in cash! And that at such a time as this when everyone is so hard up and money is so scarce. But I believe that it is a true expression of their love and appreciation for all that you and Papa have done for them.

CHAPTER NINETEEN

Between the Living and the Dead

*   *   *

Not only were people starving, but many were dying for want of medical aid. The few Chinese doctors who had been in Koon Shan before the war had left for other places where they could more safely make a living. There was malaria, typhoid, beriberi, infected wounds, skin troubles; we definitely needed a doctor.

I wrote to Mrs. Todd, my "mother in China" in Canton, who appealed to the International Red Cross. They sent us Dr. Rudolph Koch, a Jewish refugee from Vienna, under six months' contract. Naturally, he didn't know Chinese, nor did he speak much English. But the German sisters Margarete and Marie Luise could work with him, interpreting for him and helping in the treatment of the many patients who came to our improvised little clinic. We averaged 40 outpatients a day in addition to the inpatients, the sick among the Refuge children. One or two of our young Bible women trained in our own Bible school met and talked with the patients about the Lord Jesus while they were waiting to see the doctor. By this means some patients came to know Christ as their Savior.

It wasn't long before I discovered that a few women were coming to the kitchen door of the Refuge each afternoon. I inquired about them from Yan Tin who was in charge of the kitchen work.

"They are some of our neighbors from the next alley," she told me. "They used to be prosperous before the war, for they worked in the silk filatures, but now they are starving. They cannot bring themselves to go out begging, but they are getting so weak they can hardly walk. The last few afternoons they have been coming to see if there might be a little something left from the children's food that we could give them. They pick weeds in the morning and boil them without oil or salt, but they're so hungry for a few grains of rice that I have been giving them a little each time they come."

I caught a glimpse of their faces, shrunken and emaciated, skeletons of their former selves. I turned away before they came to where I would have to speak to them. I couldn't think of denying them those "few grains of rice," but I couldn't give my approval to the practice. I realized that within a few days we would have the whole town and even the surrounding villages at our doors. We took the matter to God in prayer and "Give them to eat" was the only answer we could get.

Realizing that the work of feeding adults must be done systematically if done at all, we made 100 bamboo "tickets" and gave them out through our Chinese workers to individuals who were known to be really destitute. The recipients of these tickets were told to come to the church at two in the afternoon. One of our evangelists, Mr. Cheung, was given charge of this work. The people were seated in orderly rows; then for 20 minutes or half an hour, the evangelist taught them Gospel choruses or verses of Scripture sung to Chinese tunes, making plain the way of salvation. At 2:30, men from the Children's Refuge came with big wooden buckets filled with thick, steaming hot rice soup. This was ladled into the bowl or other dish that each individual had brought with him. They waited patiently until all were served. Then the evangelist offered a short prayer of blessing, each sentence being repeated by the people. Just as soon as the Amen had been spoken, all over the room was heard the sound of sucking as that hot soup met the craving of those starving people. Their gratitude was wholehearted, but pathetic. We knew that this food wasn't enough to sustain life for any length of time.

Occasionally after the afternoon meal of soup, there would be someone too weak to drag his weary limbs back home. So he would lie on the floor of an empty building next to the church, using a broken brick for a pillow, thinking that after a night's rest he would feel able to return home. The next day or two soup would be served to him there on the floor, but by the third day he would have died. We were standing between the living and the dead, seeking to point dying souls to the Savior.

For a year and a half we kept on doing this, daily giving one hot meal to 100 persons. During that time there were two months when the number was increased to 1,000 (made possible by special gifts from Chinese Christians in Hong Kong). Five hundred were fed in Koon Shan and the remaining 500 tickets were divided between the outstations. In one place where the village elders had always been quite anti-Christian, they now cooperated in helping to keep order and persuaded some of the businessmen of the market to contribute a little so that a few more ingredients could be added to the soup.

Occasionally the Japanese military came to visit Koon Shan. Sometimes it was peaceably, sometimes with gunfire. We never knew what to expect. In August they had come with smiles. The officers had come to the Children's Refuge and looked around and had even given me 100 dollars (local currency) for the children. They evidently wanted it known that they weren't opposed to the work we were doing.

But one bright morning in early December we were startled by a sudden firing of big guns. Some of our people went to lookout points, others to places of shelter. I went to the Refuge to comfort one group of children after another, telling them not to be afraid, God had charge of us. But what was it all about? That was the question in our minds. Surely it couldn't be the Japanese. Koon Shan had been taken by them just one year previously; it was supposed to belong to them. And anyway it was more than half in ruins. What could they mean by an attack now? Yet surely the robbers had no such big guns. Perhaps the Japanese were coming for one of their visits and were just giving a warning by firing some blanks. But no, those weren't blanks: they were real shells that swirled over our heads and struck the hillside behind our house.

Presently a Japanese airplane appeared and flew so low that we could see the pilot in the cockpit. Then another plane came and bombs began to fall. We had put out our American flags at the very beginning of operations and I was glad that our two new ones were finished; I had just made one about ten feet long and the other about six. We put them out, as well as the small ones I had brought from home. They were all easily visible from the air. Eight or ten bombs were dropped altogether, five of them right in our vicinity and evidently intended for us and the Refuge.

When one of the bombs fell, it sounded so near that I wondered if it could have struck our house. I ran out from the Refuge to see. Our houses seemed to be all right, but a sort of dusty smoke was coming from the mat-shed in the playground. I ran around to the other side to investigate and saw a little blaze of fire starting from the palm-leaf roof. It was as dry as tinder and I knew there was no way to save it, but all the church benches were there. How could I let them burn? I ran back into the Refuge to find someone to help, but all were out of sight. I raced back across the playground and to the Sterling Light compound, calling for all the men to come and help save the benches. Two men, Po Tak, and two older girls put in an appearance and we started back. The airplane turned and came again just as we entered the playground. Some wanted to shrink back, but I felt strongly that their objective was accomplished now that the mat-shed was burning and the danger of bombs was over, so I rushed on into the mat-shed and the rest followed. We worked breathlessly for a few brief minutes and managed to save nearly 40 of the benches before the fire became too intense.

We then withdrew to the door of the Refuge and watched the conflagration, asking God to draw a line around that mat-shed and let nothing else be burned. Although a north wind had been blowing all night and it blew again later in the day, while the fire was burning there was perfect calm. The flames went straight up. None of the nearby buildings caught fire. Afterward, bomb splinters and pieces of shrapnel were picked up in the houses and even from the beds, yet not one of the 300 or more persons on the mission property was injured. Only the doctor, in his haste to get into the bomb shelter, had twisted his ankle and torn a ligament.

After the bombing, Japanese soldiers came into nearby villages, shooting and bayoneting anyone they met. Even the old didn't escape. In one place they rounded up the women and children and turned the machine guns on them. In another, they set fire to a house where eight or ten workmen were cooking and eating their breakfast; not one was allowed to escape. By early afternoon they were entering the east side of Koon Shan. We could mark their advance by the smoke rising from the few houses or shacks that remained along some of the streets; it seemed that they were burning each house as they came to it. I sat just inside the closed doors with my heart crying to God for wisdom and courage to face those murderers. The afternoon sun was suddenly darkened by smoke. Then they were burning to the west of us. They had passed us by! Within half an hour word was brought to us that they had gone. God had kept them from even coming to our door.

As twilight came, the wounded people of Koon Shan were brought to us on improvised stretchers. Messengers came in from the villages asking for first aid for their injured. The doctor being incapacitated by his painful ankle, the two German sisters and the Chinese nurse together with some volunteers from among our young people began rendering first aid to the injured. It took three days before they could get around to see them all. In the meantime several died and others, because of lack of early attention, developed blood poisoning and died later.

About three weeks later the Japanese came peaceably to investigate the damage they had done to our property. It seems they had thought that our mat-shed was a guerrilla meeting place. Freshly dug earth at various spots on the mountainside had looked to them like guerrilla entrenchments (they were actually places where thieves had been robbing graves looking for gold). It took hours to persuade them that no guerrillas were on our property, nor in Koon Shan, for that matter.

Our doctor's contract expired the early part of January 1940. Since that was near the end of the Chinese lunar year, a dangerous time to travel, we persuaded him to stay one more month. (All bills had to be paid by the end of the year, or go uncollected, so people were under a good deal of pressure to pay—which in turn resulted in a lot of crime.) We really would have liked to have kept him much longer, but he was getting fed up with bandits and Japanese attacks. It was evident that he was nervous about whether he would reach Canton safely, so I offered to go with him. That seemed to calm his fears. The Lord had so wonderfully preserved my "going out" and my "coming in" that many people thought I had a special guardian angel with me.

Our friend Po Luk sent two of his armed men with us for the first two or three hours of the journey by small covered rowboats through narrow winding waterways to the public motor road. When the bus came, it was already so full and so many people wanted to get on it, we didn't have a chance. At last a Japanese military truck came by, slowing down to cross a little bridge near where we were standing. Sister Marie Luise ran to it, showed her German passport, and then pointing to us said we wanted to go to Fat Shan. Using sign language, she asked if we might ride in the back of their truck. The man probably didn't understand either English or German, but after a moment's deliberation he motioned for us to climb in the back of the truck.

I called the doctor's attention to the two Japanese soldiers sitting just behind the cab with their fixed bayonets. Wasn't this the "armed foreign escort" for which he had wanted to ask the Red Cross to insure his safe conduct to Canton? We spent the night at Fat Shan and went on the next day by regular riverboat.

CHAPTER TWENTY

What You Don't Know Can Kill You

* * *

As soon as the doctor's passage to Shanghai was assured, Sister Marie Luise and I went about our errands. We seldom got to the city and had plenty to do. As the nurse, she went to the Red Cross headquarters on Shameen, the foreign concession, to get medical supplies, while I went into the Chinese city to buy toothbrushes, washcloths, soap, straps for wooden clogs, and other small things.

In charge of the Red Cross Supply Depot was a Chinese girl from Hawaii who could neither read nor speak Chinese, but had volunteered for this service. When Sister Marie Luise asked for bandages she was shown some little packages and asked if she could use them. Each package contained a bandage roll, a tiny bottle of mercurochrome, and a couple of aspirin. All of these would be useful in the Children's Refuge, so she said she would take them. Each package had some Chinese printing on the outside which looked as though it had been put on with a big rubber stamp. Although she could read Chinese, she didn't think it important to read it right then. These little packages made excellent packing between jars of ointment and bottles of solution in the big baskets. Each basket was covered with a piece of matting, sewed to the edge with string and plainly labeled in Chinese characters, "Koon Shan Children's Refuge."

It took us several days to get everything assembled and packed in 12 baskets or bundles of about 50 pounds each. We arrived at the waterfront in plenty of time, for we knew that all baggage had to be inspected by the Japanese military. However, when the Japanese saw the label "Children's Refuge," they merely motioned for us to go on the boat—no inspection necessary.

It was getting dark when we arrived in Fat Shan, and coolies swarmed onto the boat to carry baggage up to the street level. I tried to hold them back from taking our stuff until I had talked price with them. But they wouldn't talk and simply walked off up the bank with piece after piece. I hurried to follow the last one. On arriving at the street, a man's voice called me by name. By the dim light of a lantern hanging on the landing, I recognized a man from our area. He wanted to know where I was going and was all this stuff mine. A few words explained our situation. We would have to spend the night in Fat Shan and wanted a place to put all the baskets of supplies until morning when we would continue our journey.

"I have a job now working with the Japanese Water Police," he told me. "The station is right across the street; you can leave your things here with me." And he told the coolies to carry our 12 baskets across the street and stack them in a neat pile just inside the door of the Japanese Police Station.

"Now, how much do you want for your work?" I asked, turning to the coolies rather fearfully, expecting them to name a large sum.

"Don't bother to pay us," they said. "You're doing so much to help our children. We don't want your money."

I could hardly believe my ears. In my 25 years in China I'd never had coolies refuse to take payment for their work. I opened my purse and urged them to take something, but as they persistently refused, I thanked them and the man in the police station for their kindness. We were then soon on our way to spend the night with friends at the Wesleyan Mission Hospital some little distance farther along the riverbank.

The next morning we thought we were getting an early start, but our friend at the Water Police told us we should have come earlier. Then we could have had a ride on one of the Japanese military trucks. Now he would see if he could help us to get on a commercial truck. In just a short time one such truck came and the driver was willing to take us and our 12 baskets.

After about an hour we came to a river which was to be crossed by a pontoon bridge. There was a standing rule that all persons and freight must be unloaded, the truck go across empty, and the freight be carried across by a well-organized team of coolies. Japanese soldiers were there to inspect the freight. Our baskets were passed without opening. When all were loaded on the truck on the other side, I asked the head coolie how much I was to give him.

"You don't need to give us anything," he said. "You are helping our starving children. You need not pay us."

Another hour brought us to the next river where we were to go the rest of the way by boat. Again a team of coolies did the unloading and reloading, and neither they nor the truck driver would take remuneration. Perhaps their attitude caused the boatmen to be lenient with us (we had heard that this boat charged an exorbitant price for even a handbag). But when they came to collect our fares, one boatman was heard saying to another, "They don't have any freight, only a little hand luggage" (12 50-pound basketsful!). We were asked to pay only our personal fares.

It was nearly dark when we reached the waterfront at Koon Shan. Within a few minutes our own people were there to carry our baskets of supplies to the Children's

147

Refuge, while we went home and, over the supper table, told the story of the most unusual trip we'd ever experienced. As with Ezra of old, "The good hand of our God [had been] upon us" (Ezra 8: 18).

The next morning right after breakfast, I went to the Children's Refuge to get from the baskets a certain medicine for a member of our staff that was not to be put on the shelves with the other supplies. I cut the string, pulled up the matting cover of one of the baskets, and noticed the little brown paper packages used as padding between the bottles and jars. As I read the printing, my heart jumped. I broke into a cold sweat and my hands trembled as my mind raced back over the journey of the last two days— the places where the Japanese should have searched our baggage, but didn't do so—the night that those baskets had been piled up in the Japanese police station. What if someone had wondered what "those foreigners" had in all their baskets, had slipped his hand in, and gotten one of those packages?

Those packages were clearly marked for the "Chinese" army! They were a gift from overseas Chinese for the men fighting in defense of their homeland, wishing them good luck in slaughtering the enemy. Had they been found in our baskets, we would have been suspected of carrying medical supplies to the Chinese army.

A few months later I had occasion to go to Canton again on business. While there, I dropped in at the American consulate. The consul had asked me to do so when in town, for he wanted to be kept in touch with the conditions in the rural area. He stared as I told him this story.

"Well, you were fortunate," he said emphatically. "If those things had been discovered, no amount of explaining would have cleared you. Without doubt you would have had to face the firing squad."

CHAPTER TWENTY-ONE

The Squeeze Tightens

*　　*　　*

Teachers, nurses, a Chinese doctor, farmers, working men and women all came to the Children's Refuge seeking employment. If they loved our Lord, we took them in to serve for no wages other than enough to eat.

One Sunday afternoon, several hundred Japanese soldiers suddenly walked into town. Faces paled and knees weakened—but these had come peaceably. In fact, they had come to stay for a while. They went into a building at the edge of town which had formerly been occupied by one of the schools that had evacuated from Canton. They broke up the sericulture equipment which they found there, using it as fuel for cooking. During the few months they were there, the local men with guns were conspicuous by their absence.

The Japanese went to villages ten miles or more away, foraging for rice, hogs, and chickens. On one occasion a village mistook them for robbers disguised as Japanese and fired on them. One Japanese was killed and another wounded so that he died the next day. The foragers returned to Koon Shan with their dead and wounded and then the whole troop set out to take revenge. People were taken by surprise. Women and children were bayoneted in their homes and their houses set on fire and burned over them. In Koon Shan the Japanese demanded that the town supply them with several hundred weight of firewood so that they could cremate their dead. It was a time when village people were having to sell their furniture for firewood in order to have the wherewithal to keep alive.

As the year drew toward its close, we began to realize that the worst of the need had been met. There were no longer constant requests to take in more children; we had taken them all. In some cases the parents had been tided over their extreme need and now were able to take their children home. In other cases, the parents had died and the children were just left with us.

In the meantime, our Kwong Tung provincial government had opened several homes for destitute children, each accommodating a thousand. These were in Free China, a long way back from the fighting. We had been in contact with Chinese authorities from the time we first opened the Children's Refuge and they had assured us of their cooperation. Now we inquired about whether it would be possible to send some of our children to one or the other of these homes so that they could have a regular education. Thus, with the approval of parents or near relatives, we sent several groups of children across the river which divided Free China from the "occupied" area. They were met on the other side of the river by someone from the government office, given food and lodging for the night, and started on their way under friendly escort. Each one carried a Gospel of John to show them the way to eternal life and the address of their parents. A few wrote back and told us that the teachers in their new home were also Christians and that they were happy there.

The problem of keeping up the rice supply was becoming more acute. Everyone had hoped that rice harvest would bring some solution, but floods destroyed the local crop. We were still dependent on supplies coming from Canton or other places in that vicinity. As the Japanese considered our district a guerilla area, they made no effort to lessen the difficulties of obtaining food. Robbery was still prevalent on the rivers. Time and again a shipment of rice for us came through safely and then on the next day that same boat line was robbed of all its freight.

Rising costs were also a problem. In the fall of 1940, we found ourselves having to pay $140 Chinese currency a day for rice which had cost us $50 to $70 a few months earlier. These facts influenced our decision to cut down where possible on the number of children in the Refuge. They also made us turn our thoughts to Free China where rice was much cheaper and more readily obtainable. This resulted in my taking a trip to Shiu Hing, the first city of any size up the West River. There I contacted the authorities and they gave me a permit to buy rice and transport it back to Koon Shan. This was prohibited for Chinese civilians, but was allowed for our Children's Refuge.

In March 1941 I had to go to Canton to attend to business matters and buy supplies. I hadn't been to the city for eight months since more recently the German sisters had taken over this responsibility. All went well until I was on the riverboat starting back with ten baskets and bundles of supplies. There was no trouble in boarding the boat at the regular landing, but when we came to a suburb of the city, the boat stopped and Japanese police boarded it to inspect passengers and baggage. They asked me to show my travel pass. I showed them my passport which was the only document I had ever needed in my previous trips to the city. But the gendarmes would not accept it now. They insisted I have a travel pass before I could go any farther.

"But I have ten pieces of baggage here," I argued, "How can I go back to get a pass now?"

"You must hire a rowboat to take you back to the city, baggage and all" was the decisive answer.

151

There was no way to get out of it. The police wouldn't allow the boat to go with me on it and the captain said it was high time to be on the way. A little rowboat was called, my ten pieces of baggage loaded into it, and I on top of them. I didn't like being turned back. I wondered what it all meant. I had never been asked for a travel pass before; why should they demand one now?

The little boat took me to the South China Boat Mission where I left my ten pieces of luggage with our good friends while I hurried on into the city, hoping to get my pass in time to catch the afternoon boat to Fat Shan en route to Koon Shan. But the Japanese officials had different ideas. They asked many questions and then told me to come back for my pass in three days. I fretted under the delay, but kept looking to the Lord to know what His plan in the matter was.

When I presented myself at the appointed hour on the third day, I was met by a stern Japanese army officer who had for his interpreter an officious young chap who had grown up in the United States. The officer explained to me through the interpreter that a state of war existed between China and the Imperial Army (as if I didn't know it!) and that they very much disliked having persons of third nationalities traveling in and out of Canton City. He informed me that the next time I wished to come from Koon Shan to Canton, I must first notify the American consul. He in turn would notify them and then I must wait until they granted permission.

"If you do not comply with this order of procedure and come without permission, you are liable to arrest. Do you understand?"

"Yes," I mumbled and nodded my head with some form of respect, but inwardly I was thinking, "That settles it; I'll not come back to Canton until you are all gone!"

As soon as I arrived back in Koon Shan, I called a

meeting of the staff and church committee to announce that I felt it was time to move our Children's Refuge to the interior, away from the Japanese-occupied area. Opinions varied: some thought it entirely unnecessary, some thought it might not be a bad idea, but that there was no hurry about it. We could arrive at no decision ourselves, so we asked the Lord to decide for us.

Some of us would cross the river into Free China and look for a place where we could house 100 children. We made two stipulations: the location must be north of the West River and must be in an area where rice was grown so that we wouldn't have to depend on transportation for our staple food supply. We prayed that if God, who knows the future, didn't want us to move away from our old location, He would let us find only closed doors; but that if He did want us to go to the interior, He would make it plain by opening a door for us in the place of His selection.

With this prayer in our hearts, a little group of us set out and crossed the river boundary between the Japanese-occupied area (in which we had been living for over two years) and Free China. Instead of the desolation, hardship, and tension of the occupied territory, here were freedom and normal life, children going to school, chickens and pigs in the streets. The leisurely congeniality that was characteristic of the Chinese was prevalent everywhere, even among the soldiers who guarded the riverbank.

We spent the first night in a little inn at a town only a short distance from the river where we had crossed. The next morning we were up early, cooked and ate our rice at the inn, and were ready at 7:30 to set out on what we thought would be a 15-mile walk. It had rained in the night. The paths in that district were not paved with stone slabs as were those back in Sai Chiu; they were just mud, sticky in some places, slippery in others. After five hours of steady, brisk walking we arrived at the place where we had been told a motorboat was running. Now we learned that it hadn't been running for some days; nothing to do but walk the remaining ten miles. The mud was worse than ever, but we plodded on. It was half past four in the afternoon when we finally arrived at the point on the West River where boats were available to take us to Shiu Hing. One of our party was nearly exhausted. Another said he'd never in his life been so tired. I had a raw spot on my heel as big as a half dollar. But we were happy and thankful that it hadn't rained at all while we were walking.

In Shiu Hing we visited the chief executive who had thirteen counties under his jurisdiction. I had met him on a previous trip to Shiu Hing. He was friendly toward our work among the children. In fact, it was he who had given me the permit to buy rice in Free China to take to the Refuge. When we told him our errand, he agreed that it would be wise to move, but advised our going farther from the frontier to look for a place. The next town up the river was Luk Po, the hometown of Mr. Lei who had been so long associated with us in the work in Koon Shan. But now at Luk Po everything was occupied by the Chinese military.

At the suggestion of friends there, we took an 11-mile walk over a range of mountains to the northwest of Luk Po, which brought us to a market town in a rich valley. There we made inquiries which resulted in our taking to the road again to contact the District Officer. The additional two hours' walk to Wing Fung Shi held a new experience for us. At several places the shallow, sandy-bottomed river or its tributaries had to be crossed by narrow footbridges. These bridges were less than 15 inches wide and were supported on posts 10 or 12 feet above the riverbed. There were no railings. Two of these bridges were 80 or 100 yards in length. We found ourselves almost holding our breath until we got across. I reminded the

Lord that somewhere in His Word He had said something about keeping the feet of His saints and I asked Him please to do so now.

The District Officer was kind and offered us the use, rent free, of as many shop buildings in Wing Fung Shi as we might need to house the children. It was a rice-raising district and also north of the West River. We couldn't doubt that God had opened the door.

The buildings were of mud brick and had only earth floors, but they did have lofts, reached by ladders, which could be used for dormitories, while ground floors would do well for classrooms and dining room.

CHAPTER TWENTY-TWO

The Pacific Is Closed!

*   *   *

We returned to Koon Shan and reported the result of our trip. Our staff and the other missionaries agreed that it was evidently God's plan for us to make the move to Wing Fung Shi. We put in our request to the authorities in Shiu Hing for the necessary pass to move across the river. There were delays; Chinese officialdom did not work quickly as a rule and we learned lessons in patience. In the meantime, the price of rice in the occupied area was rising. We found that it was costing $4,000 (Chinese currency) for rice that over in Free China would be only $1,500 a month. More lessons in patience.

At last everything was packed up, the permit was in hand, a junk had been engaged on the West River to take us to a point where the overland route would be the shortest, and we set out: 51 children and 19 adults (teachers, nurses, cooks, and water-carrier) plus 110 pieces of baggage. The whole distance was probably only 90 miles, but it took about six days for the children to get there. We traveled by seven different boats for long or short distances, interspersed with cross-country walks. The walks presented a motley picture: 55 carrier loads of baggage, 14 children too small to walk the distance, each in a big rice basket on shoulder poles, 23 children and 17 adults who walked, and two carrying chairs for women who couldn't walk so far. The hearts of people all along the way were touched and everyone was kind to us. Two or three of the work women and I left the party at Luk Po and walked the 22 miles through the mountains to get there first and do some house cleaning.

The District Officer continued to be kind and helpful in many ways. His office was just next door to the building that we used for dining room and kitchen and where my sleeping quarters were in the loft. He dropped in two or three times a day, just to see that we had all we needed and that everything was all right.

We had two big rice kettles (about a yard in diameter) but there was a fireplace for only one of them. He therefore put his men to work building another fireplace of mud brick to fit our other kettle. Then a cover was needed for that kettle, so he went to the carpenter shop up the street and gave orders for a cover to be made to fit it, like an inverted washtub. He occasionally came to our Sunday services.

One day he said, "I ought to be a Christian; I belonged to the YMCA when I was in Canton." Then he hastily added, "But you wouldn't have me in the church; I have six wives!" He kept a wife in each town that he had to frequent on business. That eliminated hotel bills!

In July of 1941 I made another trip back to Koon Shan to get a few more older children who were to attend junior high school in the interior. We crossed the river without the Japanese knowing we had come and gone. Two days later the Japanese military moved up the east bank of the river, occupying all the little towns along the way and declaring the river "closed." No one was to cross it. But the children and I were safely over in Free China.

In October I had letters from the German sisters in Koon Shan telling me they hoped that in some way I would be able to come back there at the end of the month for the yearly meeting. Many decisions had to be made about how to carry on the work. They knew that the river was closed and advised going by way of Hong Kong and Canton if necessary.

This latter suggestion did not appeal to me at all. In the first place, I didn't have the means for making so circuitous a trip. Nor did I have suitable clothes. (My Chinese clothes were inappropriate for a sophisticated city like Hong Kong.)

So I made inquiries of friends in Shiu Hing who had come from Koon Shan. They told me that Chinese guerrillas were crossing the river every night to smuggle kerosene into Free China and they assured me that I could get safely across with them.

I took with me a young woman who had graduated from our Bible school and Mr. Lei's son, who was ready for college; they were young and strong, good walking companions. Both were temporarily helping in the children's work.

It was a long walk from Shiu Hing through mud and rain to the little town near the river crossing. From there we were directed to be at the riverbank just before dark. When we got there, a few little boats had already pulled out from the shore and one was there to take us.

On arriving at the other side, we were having a little difficulty finding our way in the dark. Turning the corner of a field of tall sugarcane, we were suddenly accosted by a man with a gun. It took only a moment for him to establish our identity and then he was as cordial as could be. He was a well-known guerrilla chieftain and he greeted me as the "great benefactor of Sai Chiu." At first he offered us the hospitality of his home for the night, but when he found we wanted to get back to Koon Shan, he sent one of his men to get us safely through the village and out onto the path that would lead "home."

What a surprise our German sisters and the rest of our folks had when about half past nine that night they answered to the pounding on the gate of Sterling Light Garden to find that I had come back and at such a time of night! Back in "the good old days" before the war, we had always made it a point to be home before dark. In wartime we had now crossed the river and walked two hours in the dark! It was only by the good hand of our God.

Later, a Monday in December 1941 I had occasion to stop in at the Kwong Tung Provincial Bank in Shiu Hing to see the manager. He was a Christian man and very friendly. In the course of our conversation, I mentioned that an American missionary there, Mrs. Burtt, was expecting to return to the States and wanted me to go the first part of the way to Hong Kong with her.

"Oh!" he exclaimed. "She cannot go. The Japanese have attacked Hong Kong, and declared war on the United States and Great Britain. The Pacific is closed."

When I asked him how he knew (there were no newspapers in Shiu Hing), he told me he'd received a telegram the previous day from the bank's headquarters in Kukong. It was a fact: the United States was in the war. That changed things; Mrs. Burtt had to drop her plans for going home and I wouldn't be able to make another trip to Koon Shan for years.

About two weeks later I had a letter from Sister Margarete, sent by the "underground," telling of the most recent visit of the Japanese military. It was on the 9th of December and there were 300 of them. The few residents of the town became very frightened at the sight; no one knew whether they were coming peaceably or to slaughter them. But it was soon evident that they had a definite objective. They came straight to our mission property, surrounded it, and set guards with fixed bayonets at each gate. A heavy machine gun was carried in and set down on the path

160

facing the front door. Some officers stomped into the house, expecting to find me, an objectionable American, and put me into concentration camp. But I wasn't there.

Sister Margarete was the only one at home that day, Sister Marie Luise having gone to Fat Shan to see if she could do anything to help our English friends in charge of the Wesleyan Mission Hospital. Margarete met them as they came in and then spent hours answering their grilling questions. Every niche, corner, and cupboard was searched and searched again.

"If she is here and you are deceiving us, we will behead you!" one of the officers threatened.

At last they had to accept disappointment. If they couldn't get hold of the American, they would have the property. They ordered the American flag taken down from its pole on the orphanage building and a Japanese flag put in its place.

"This all belongs to the Imperial Army now," they said. "Nothing may be taken from this property. It is ours."

But they went away without taking inventory. They had scarcely left the town before Mr. Lei went to the local "puppet" authorities (village men who held these positions with the Japanese merely to avert a massacre of their village people) and asked whether they intended to carry out the orders that the military had just given about the mission property. They assured him that they did not and that our people were free to do anything they chose with what was on the premises. Consequently my winter clothing and bedding which I hadn't taken were sent to me when I needed them; also books and other things arrived, all by way of the "underground." The military never came back to claim "their" possessions. Probably they thought they weren't worth it, or perhaps they forgot.

In the meantime the sisters went on with their work in Koon Shan. The Japanese had no enmity for them. There

161

was still much to be done there and they kept on all through the remaining years of the war, ministering to the suffering, witnessing to the dying, comforting the broken-hearted, and encouraging the Chinese church in its struggle to keep on going when the war had deprived them of so much. When the war was over I came back from the mountain districts and found everything just as it had been when I left four years before.

CHAPTER TWENTY-THREE

The Market of Eternal Plenty

* * *

Shortly after getting settled in Wing Fung Shi, the District Officer came to me one day saying that he wanted to inquire about the organization we were connected with. Who was responsible for our support? I told him that we looked to God to supply our needs. God caused people to send gifts for the work, people in the United States or even in Hong Kong, without our asking them to give.

"That's no way to run a work like this!" he had exclaimed emphatically. "It takes a lot of rice to feed all these children."

I told him I knew a lot of rice was needed, but I told him God also knew and was able to supply it. He shook his head and was about to walk away when I called him back.

"Listen!" I said. "Suppose you sent one or two of your men down to Tak Hing City on a matter of business for you, a matter that might take a week or ten days to accomplish. Would they have to worry about whether they would have enough to eat while there?"

"Of course not!" he exclaimed.

"Why?" I asked.

"I would be responsible, of course!"

"All right," I said. "You are a reliable man; you can be counted on to live up to your responsibilities. What about the God who made heaven and earth? Isn't He reliable? Can't He be counted on? It is God who has given us this work to do for Him, taking care of these children. Why should I worry about their not having enough to eat?"

"Oh, well, if you put it that way . . ." He had gone out shaking his head.

Returning from Shui Hing I again trudged along the mountain paths and forded the rivers. Having learned of the new turn the war had taken, I wondered what it would mean. Now America was involved. How would it affect us? The last part of the way I was walking alone. I had a little book of the Psalms in Chinese set to music which I almost always carried with me on these long walks. We enjoyed singing them on the lonely parts of the way. That afternoon the words of the first two verses of Psalm 25 were uppermost in my mind, "Unto thee, O Lord, do I lift up my soul. O my God, I trust in thee: let me not be ashamed." But the Chinese version has that last sentence, "I shall not be ashamed." I reminded the Lord of how I had made my boast in Him to the District Officer; now I was still trusting and it was up to Him to keep us from having to be ashamed. Once again I sensed assurance and peace.

On my arrival at the Children's Refuge, one of the women from the kitchen provided me with a basin of hot water (a custom of those mountain villagers) to wash my feet. I sat on a little low stool in the room just behind the dining room, enjoying the relaxation and refreshment of the hot water, when I heard the skeptical District Officer's voice in the dining room. There was no time to get my shoes back on nor even to stand up, for within seconds he was at the door between the two rooms. He was a large man and almost completely filled the doorway. I tried to apologize for not standing up to greet him properly, but he didn't wait to hear what I was trying to say.

"Now what are you going to do? he blurted out. "The

war has come to Hong Kong; no more banking there. The Pacific is closed; no more ships; no more mail."

"Just what we have been doing," I replied, smiling at his evident intense concern for us and the children.

"And what is that?" he asked, apparently having forgotten our former conversation.

"Trusting God," I replied. "The bank of Heaven isn't closed by the war. God has other routes than just by the Pacific. I don't know how He will provide, but He will."

Again he turned and went back to his office shaking his head. This crazy little American woman just didn't have sense enough to know how much rice it would take to continue to feed all those children, especially when there was a war on. Some months later he was transferred to another part of the province. On leaving, he told us he was sorry to go. He had hoped that if he stayed on, he might be able to help us when we might come to want. At intervals during the next year or so one of the officer's underlings who was a mountain village man would come back to visit his family. On these trips he always came first to the Children's Refuge to ask about our welfare, saying that the officer had sent him to see that we were all right. We always assured him that our God was taking care of us.

Although the name of the place where we had come to live, Wing Fung Shi, meant Market of Eternal Plenty, it could hardly be claimed that our food supplies were always plentiful. Rice was our staple, taking the place of both bread and potatoes. Each person was limited to two bowls of rice a meal. The bigger boys had bigger bowls and the smaller children had smaller bowls, but the one rule held for adults as well as for children. When we first went there to live, no vegetables were available in the market. The people of the surrounding villages were all farmers, but each family grew only the vegetables they wanted for themselves. When they saw that we wanted vegetables, they planted more and brought them to sell in the market. Meat was available only every third day, on "market day" and we didn't always have the money. The two commodities in abundance were garlic and black pickled beans.

During the second year at Wing Fung Shi we bought a little pig to raise. We fed it on bran mixed with the water in which our rice was washed. It grew quickly so that at Christmastime it furnished us with enough meat for our family of 150 to have two days of pork with our rice. We sold enough to buy another piglet and start over.

I had one of those old-fashioned books that has recipes and instructions for doing almost everything. In it were instructions for making bacon. According to the instructions, I took two pieces of the side meat, rubbed them well with salt, brown sugar, and a bit of saltpeter, sewed them up in porous bags and hung them on the wall in the kitchen high above our rice kettles. We burned grass for fuel to cook our rice, so twice a day there was plenty of smoke. After about a month or more, we tried the bacon and found it was delicious. Somehow I found a way by the "underground" to send one piece of it to Koon Shan to the German sisters. In due time I had a letter from them saying they had never eaten such good bacon, no, not even in Germany! It was perhaps just that we had so little of anything that tasted like home, that the little we did have tasted especially good.

That old-fashioned book was good for many things. Some of the children got coughs. One of the lofts where the boys slept was right next to mine, with just a thin board partition between. I heard how much they coughed before going to sleep at night. The book said that a syrup made of pine needles and sugar was a good remedy. Pine needles were plentiful there in the mountains and native brown sugar was inexpensive. We cooked up a big kettleful of the mixture and gave each boy a bowlful, hot and steaming, just before they went to bed. They liked it and it did the trick. After about three treatments, their coughing stopped.

Two or three of the little boys developed what the Chinese call "chicken blindness." Just after sundown they could be seen groping their way around when it was still light enough for everyone else to see clearly where they were going. Halibut oil, or anything like it, was not to be had even in the city of Shiu Hing. But the village nearest to the market had a small fish pond. Since some of the women of the village had become very friendly with us, we persuaded them to let us have a fish perhaps once a week out of their pond. The entrails of the fish were carefully cleaned, steamed on the top of the rice and served to the boys who had trouble seeing after sundown. A few such meals produced the desired effect: the boys could see all right. (Fish entrails cooked with egg were considered a delicacy by many of the Chinese of our area.)

In the late fall of our second year in Wing Fung Shi, the District Officer informed us of a wartime law requiring anyone who owned land which they didn't utilize during the winter months to make it available for anyone who wanted to plant winter crops. He called our attention to the fact that the fields all around us produced two crops of rice a year and then lay idle for three or four months. He told us we could have as much land as we could work. When the children heard about it they were enthusiastic. The boys took one field and the girls another, competing to produce the best vegetables or most potatoes. One year we raised about a ton of potatoes. To be sure, they were small. They had to be dug the first of March before they were fully grown in order to return the field to its owners to prepare for the spring rice planting. But they were our own potatoes and they did taste good.

When we had moved to Wing Fung Shi early in the

summer of 1941, there had been no Christian work nearer than at Luk Po, down on the West River, 22 miles away. I had told the children and their teachers and nurses that it was like going to open a new outstation of the mission, only that instead of having one preacher and perhaps a Bible woman, there were 51 of us who must witness for the Lord by our lives as well as by our words. We lived openly before the people of those mountain villages. Our doors were always open, except at night. When we ate our meals, a crowd often gathered at the door to watch. They marveled at the children's good behavior. We invited them to attend our services on Sundays, but they were shy about coming in. On the road to Luk Po we often got into conversation with the people as we walked along or sat with them for rest and refreshment at the tea stations. We gave them tracts and told them of the Savior and His love. A few had heard before, but to the great majority it was all new and strange.

Not long after our move, conditions in the Japanese-occupied district became worse and worse. Some Christian girls in Wa Ha who were self-employed in silk-making began to despair. They considered selling their silk looms for firewood. But Mr. Lei suggested that we somehow move these girls and their four looms up to Luk Po in Free China, where they could continue their weaving. This wasn't easy, but it was accomplished. In time the silk material they produced helped tide the mission over when our funds from other sources were completely cut off.

Now and again new children were brought to us from the Japanese-occupied areas. We would meet these in Shiu Hing, travel with them by the night boat to Luk Po (the boats traveled at night because of the danger of bombing in the daytime), and then set out early the next morning for the long walk through the mountains. When we had small children with us, we didn't try to go more than ten or sixteen miles in one day; we could spend the night with Christian friends in villages when necessary. But even those distances were a good deal for the legs of children already weakened from undernourishment. We let them have time for a little rest at every good stopping place. But when I would see one who was getting too tired, I would stoop down, saying, "Want a ride?" and then take the child on my back. After some distance of the mountin path had been covered, she would be refreshed; perhaps she had even had a little nap on my back. I would let her slide to the ground and take up another little fellow who was finding his feet too heavy to keep going. And this little act, a tangible evidence of the love of God, bore its testimony to the people of those mountain villages.

The longer we stayed in Wing Fung Shi, the more strongly we felt that God had brought us there for a purpose other than just to have a safe place for our children's work. He had used this as a means to bring us into that mountainous back country in order to open up new evangelistic work.

One of the Bible women who had worked with us in the Koon Shan area was a basket weaver. We had her join us at Wing Fung Shi for two reasons: she could teach our boys to weave baskets and could help in giving out the Gospel to the village people. When the village elder knew that we wanted to buy bamboo for weaving baskets, he gave us a letter of introduction to a man who had a bamboo grove in a mountain canyon a short distance to the north. Two or three of the boys, the Bible woman, and I set out to find it. We really didn't know the way, but the Lord let us join a man who was going the same way. As he showed us the way to the mountain canyon, we showed him the way to eternal life.

The letter of introduction brought us a cordial reception and we had no trouble getting the bamboo we wanted. At the house where the bamboo was weighed and paid for in the entrance to the narrow canyon, the people were so friendly we had a little talk with them and offered them a Gospel of John. They gladly accepted it and promised to read it. They even asked us to spend the night with them and tell them more of this "Good News."

Once during the Chinese New Year festivities, a Bible woman and I spent from one to three days in each of three mountain villages. In one of these were several people who called themselves Christians, but who were such hard-working people and so far away from any place for Christian meetings that they were almost starved for Christian teaching and fellowship. We had Bible studies with them mornings and afternoons and evenings.

In another of those villages one young man had recently become a Christian. He wanted his folks to hear the Good News which had made such a change in him. We arrived there late in the afternoon and after the first words of greeting, the people began asking questions. We started telling of God's love in sending His Son into the world to save us. Supper was soon ready so those who weren't of the immediate family withdrew to their own homes while we ate. But the dishes had scarcely been cleared away when neighbors and relatives crowded into the big living room eager to hear more. It was well into the night when at last our hosts insisted that it was time for us to stop and have a cup of tea before retiring. The next morning it was the same. Immediately after tea and New Year's goodies, the crowd was there waiting to hear what we had to say. All day long they kept us talking, one of us and then the other, with intervals for the two meals of rice and an occasional snack. It was a time of seed-sowing and we prayed earnestly that some seed might fall on good soil so that it would bring forth fruit for the glory of God.

In the third village we had only a day and one night, but

170

the listeners again were alert and eager. On the way home to Wing Fung Shi, a distance too great to be covered in one day, we stopped overnight with a middle-aged couple in a little isolated village. While we were eating supper the man said that the people of the village had almost never seen a foreigner, so they would like to hear what I had to say. He intimated that I could speak to them from his front door, as his house was too small to accommodate the crowd. I told him I would be glad to speak to them for a little while, but that I had almost no voice left after all the speaking I had been doing the past few days. I said I had about ten copies of the Gospel of John left and would offer them for sale. They could read them for themselves. My hostess snorted at the idea of offering something for sale.

"The people of this village," she said emphatically, "are so wicked they won't buy anything Christian!"

I made no other reply than just to smile at her, but inwardly I lifted my heart to God in prayer. When supper was over, I went to the front door. The crowd gathered and I gave a short Gospel message, making it as simple and as plain as I knew how. Then I offered them the Gospels of John, telling them these little books were the Word of God and that they told more fully of His love to us. I offered them for one dollar apiece. (That was during the time of inflation and one dollar was the smallest denomination in current use at the time.) I was at once almost overwhelmed by hands thrusting dollar bills into mine and taking one of the little books. All ten copies were gone in a moment and those who didn't get one were almost cross with me because I didn't have more.

Inflation was upon us. Chinese currency was depreciating daily, and prices rising accordingly. The worst of it was that the government had pegged the rate of the American dollar, so it was being dragged downward with the national currency. When we had opened the Children's

Refuge in 1939, one American dollar would feed a child for a month. By 1943 it took twenty dollars. But without our seeking it, the Lord brought us into contact with China's Children Fund (now called Christian Children's Fund) and they offered to assume support for 50 of our children, a great help. By that time we had about 140 children with us in Wing Fung Shi and the expense of feeding them was just around $1,000 dollars national currency a day. Well-meaning friends and even some staff members advised giving up the children.

"But how can we give them up?" I remonstrated. "They have no homes to which to go, no one to care for them. We can't simply turn them out on the streets and let them starve. God doesn't do things halfway; I believe He will see us through."

And He did. A Chinese Relief Committee in Kukong helped with a generous donation every month in addition to what the CCF was giving us. Funds from America were able to come through the Bank of China and the Chinese government added 50 percent to all gifts sent for relief work. Later they even raised their subsidy to 100 percent. These funds, however, couldn't be remitted directly to Wing Fung Shi. The amounts from Kulong came to the bank in Shiu Hing and those from America to the bank in Wuchow. This necessitated my making frequent trips to either one or the other of these cities. These trips meant either the 22-mile walk down through the mountains to Luk Po on the West River, a wait until about midnight for the boat, then a four-hour boat ride downriver to Shiu Hing; or eight hours upriver to Wuchow, transact the business in the city, back on the boat the next night for return to Luk Po, and then again the long walk through the mountains back to Wing Fung Shi with the precious money to supply the children with their food.

These riverboats were of the same type of structure with

which I had become acquainted on my first arrival in China, only there were no longer the private "cubby holes." At the rear of the ship, down low, was what was called the "public hold" where both men and women could ride. This compartment was brightly lighted with an air-pressure lamp; there were three tiers of bunks. The lowest was on a level with the floor, the second and third being like big six-foot-wide shelves protruding inward from the side walls of the boat. The shelves were covered with clean matting and divided off into individual spaces about thirty inches wide by boards that stood four or five inches high. The compartment accommodated about 60 passengers. In the open space in the middle of the room were a table and a few chairs. An attendant was always on duty. For hours during the first part of the night there were always medicine sellers haranguing the passengers about the excellent qualities of their particular medicine.

Immediately above this compartment was what was known as the "dining room" which was considered strictly first class. There were only two tiers of bunks and perhaps the matting on them was a little cleaner. There were outside windows and more space around the table. I usually traveled in the public hold, but frequently when boarding the boat at Luk Po I would find the place already full to capacity so I would go up to the dining room to find that even there the bunks were all full. So I would have to spend the night sitting on a stiff bamboo stool.

One trip of that sort a month wasn't bad at all, but during the time of very high prices (1943) when every remittance was utilized to the full as soon as it was received, it became necessary to go three or even four times a month. Sometimes when walking through the dark streets of Luk Po to board a boat, or just having disembarked from one, I would think of the people sleeping in the houses I passed. I almost envied them, being able to sleep in their own beds every night while I was sitting up on a crowded boat or finishing out the night on a bench in the church. But then my thoughts turned to the One who said, "The Son of man hath not where to lay his head," and it brought such a joyous feeling of fellowship with Him that it set my heart singing.

In the long hours on the boat at night when the bright lights and the haranguing of the medicine vendors kept me from sleeping, I loved to meditate on the Lord's words, "Abide in me." I took them to mean "Dwell in me" or "Make me your home" and in that sense I could always be at home, whether on the mountain or the riverboat. I was in Him, in my home, and in that home was everything I needed: living water, bread of life, light, and rest.

These trips also afforded opportunity for witnessing to all sorts of people, mostly men. Once it was to a group of new recruits for the army, another to two men in chains being taken to prison. Sometimes it was to officials or well-to-do businessmen, and occasionally to the few women who traveled by those night boats.

For the long walk through the mountains God had provided a walking companion of His own choice. A group of about ten boys had been sent to us from Sai Ch'iu; among them was Ah Hei, a 16-year-old, too old to be received in the Refuge. But the one who sent the group to us asked that we find some place where this boy could get employment, for in the Japanese-occupied area he would starve to death. He had been with us only a day or two when we found that he was a very capable boy, so our staff was unanimous in deciding to keep him as a helper. In due time he was assigned to accompany me on my trips to Luk Po and Shiu Hing. He was indeed a godsend. No matter how hot in summer, how cold in winter, how heavy the rain, or how muddy the path, he never complained, but was always happy, smiling, and helpful.

CHAPTER TWENTY-FOUR

In the Shadow of His Hand

* * *

In 1944 prices dropped somewhat—just why, we never knew, for we had no newspapers or radio—but it was a welcome change. Our money went further and lasted longer. There were not so many trips to the banks. But we heard rumors that something was impending. Letters from the U. S. ambassador in Kunming advised all American citizens in the West River area to evacuate. Mrs. Burtt left Shiu Hing and went to Wuchow, for she heard that a plane was flying from there to Kunming. Friends in Tak Hing wrote me that they would be leaving within a week; wouldn't I come with them? I laid that letter before the Lord, asking Him to show me clearly what I should do. There was no "green light" to go, but there was peace and assurance about staying; I let the others go without me.

Shortly after that I had two reasons for making a trip to Shiu Hing: Mrs. Burtt wrote from India with a message for me to pass on to the Chinese woman she had left in charge of her blind school, and notice came from the bank in Shiu Hing that a remittance had been received there for me. As I was planning to go, one of our teachers told me that just that day a good many soldiers had passed through a neighboring village. No one seemed to know where they came from nor where they were going, but something seemed to be in the air. She warned me to make careful inquiries as I went, adding, "We don't want you running into any danger."

I thanked her for her concern and after retiring that night I thought and prayed over what she had said. I realized that if the Japanese should come into that district it wouldn't be best for me to stay in Wing Fung Shi. There were too many outlaws in the mountains who, if they found that it would be to their profit to hand me over to the Japanese, wouldn't hesitate to do so. Could it be that our happy village life was to be interrupted now by an invasion of the enemy? When I packed my knapsack I slipped in two or three extra items that might be convenient to have in case my trip should be longer than the planned three days. I also whispered to the woman in charge of the kitchen where among the things in my room she would find money for daily expenses when the three days' supply I had already given her might be used up.

In Wing Fung Shi we had next to nothing in the way of furniture in our living quarters. In the dining room the long tables and benches consisted of heavy planks supported by pedestals of mud bricks. In the dormitories most of us slept right on the floorboards. I was one of the few who had a bed (boards resting on two sawhorses). There were no closets, cupboards, drawers. Everything—clothing, bedding, books and papers—were kept in the sacks in which they had been moved from Koon Shan. In my case, these were stored under my bed. It was a matter of telling my helper in which sack she would find the money.

It was a hot, wilting day in September when we left. We got an early start on the road as soon as it was light enough to see. As our path wound in and out among the mountains, the melody of "Guide me, O Thou great Jehovah" kept singing itself through my mind. I couldn't recall the correct words of the song, but the words which seemed to fit the tune were, "Hide me, O Thou great

Jehovah, in the shadow of Thy hand." And as I realized what I had sung, I wondered if I was going to need hiding.

We had walked about half of the distance when we began to meet people who told us that the Japanese were coming, but they couldn't give any definite information. We kept on our way. The nearer we drew to Luk Po, the more people we met; they were evacuating, taking their belongings with them. They looked at me wonderingly.

"Why are you going to Luk Po?" some asked me. "We are leaving; the 'little Japs' are coming."

I had no good answer to give them, but still I went on. The house belonging to Mr. Lei and his wife in Luk Po faced on the mulberry fields at the back of the town. I went directly there without having to pass through any of the streets. They welcomed me warmly, but the look of anxiety on their faces let me know how real the trouble was. The Japanese were advancing; they might be in Shiu Hing, only 18 miles away, that day. It was quickly decided that I should pick up my things at the church—bed mat, blanket, and mosquito net—and go back five or six miles into the mountains to stay at the home of their married daughter.

On the way down from Wing Fung Shi that day, I had made a misstep and strained the tendons in the arch of my left foot. It had caused me only a little discomfort while walking the rest of the way, but when I had been sitting with my friends in Luk Po for a little while, I found it caused a great deal of pain to put my foot on the floor. So while I was treating my foot with hot water and turpentine, Ah Hei, the boy who was my walking companion, went to the church and gathered my belongings for me. It was a small incident, but God had His hand in it. We learned later that Japanese spies were already in the town that day. Had they seen me in the streets, the military, when they came, would doubtless have searched for me until they found me. The Japanese had announced when they started their big drive westward that they were after the British and Americans. But God was already hiding me "in the shadow of His hand."

By the time our bundles were packed, I was able to walk and we went to the friends in the mountains where we could still keep in touch with what was going on. A few days later, the Japanese were actually coming into Luk Po. Mr. and Mrs. Lei joined me and we withdrew to their tiny native village near the top of the mountains, five or six miles away. We soon felt that the village was too near the road for safety, too easily observed by passersby. There was a little cabin about 20 minutes' climb from the village among the woods on the side of the mountain. It was hidden from view by the trees. I went there to stay.

Two days later the Japanese troops began passing on the other side of the ravine; I could see them through the trees and hear their voices as they shouted to one another. They continued passing at intervals for a week or more. While they were actually passing the whole village, perhaps ten people joined me in my hiding place, but when immediate danger was over they returned to their houses and fields. I stayed there for two months. Food supplies (mainly rice) were brought to me from the village and I enjoyed a real vacation in the out-of-doors. What did I do? I read the Bible, learned more of the thousands of Chinese characters, and helped Mrs. Lei with sewing. I cooked and washed. We had one small box of matches and decided to limit ourselves to one match a day, so it was necessary to continually gather pine cones to keep the fire going. Of course we didn't venture out at night because of tigers.

Most of the time I had two or three companions: Mr. and Mrs. Lei who had been with us in the work so many years and a teenage niece of theirs who had been in our orphanage primary school. That village was Mr. Lei's

178

birthplace and all the people in it were related to him in some way. God had provided that hiding place for me.

In the meantime our children and their teachers had varied experiences. On the first Sunday after I had left them, they had the joy of baptizing four young converts in the river. Two were local women who had found the Lord and for two years had given evidence of being believers. The other two were members of our Children's Refuge. Although that Sunday morning had begun with this happy event, there were rumors in the air that caused our staff no little anxiety. They held a meeting that evening to discuss what they would do in case the Japanese should really come to their little out-of-the-way place.

The following morning at early roll call they were instructing the children about what should be done in case of an invasion when a messenger rushed into the village with the warning that the Japanese were an hour down the road. Their words had to be put immediately into action. The most necessary things were hurriedly stuffed into sacks for the bigger boys to carry. The teachers and all children over ten years of age were evacuated to a place farther back in the mountains where the villagers gave them refuge until the danger was past. Only the smaller children were left with a few of the oldest work women to care for them; one woman teacher chose to stay.

The Japanese troops came to Wing Fung Shi, helped themselves to whatever they wanted from the shops and houses, spent a night, and went on the next morning. This continued for four days.

When the last installment came, very little was left for them to take; they were tired, dirty, and half sick so they didn't want to carry their own gear. In the morning when they left they took with them ten of our little boys to carry small loads for them; they also took the four old work women and the woman teacher. None of them was used to carrying loads or to walking long distances; it didn't seem possible that they would ever come back alive. But our God is able to do abundantly above all that we ask or think. The women carried their loads for two days, keeping their places in the line up and down the steep rough mountains, through streams and across muddy fields.

On the morning of the third day, the Japanese officer spoke to them and by the use of signs asked if they were Christians. They smilingly replied that they were and he then made signs to the effect that they were allowed to return. Some camp followers who could speak Chinese warned them not to return by the same route lest they be taken by other troops. A small quantity of rice was given to each for food by the way. Heeding the warning, they avoided the path, keeping to the hilltops, but they lost their way. They met with robbers, but used it as an opportunity to witness for the Lord. Nights were spent in the open out on the mountainsides, in a district where tigers weren't unknown. They were four days on the return trip and arrived in Wing Fung Shi, not only no worse for the experience, but even stronger physically and full of praise to God for the way He had cared for them.

Although the women were allowed to come back, we were unable to locate the boys until the war was over. One of them had found his way to Hong Kong; two others were in Canton and still others were in towns along the West River where the Japanese had dropped them.

After two months of living in the cabin in the woods, I realized it was time to find some way of contacting the outside world. The funds we had in hand when the Japanese had come up the West River weren't going to last much longer. Shiu Hing was now in the hands of the enemy; no banking could be done there. But where to go was the question.

At the beginning of my stay at the cabin when I was

looking to the Lord for guidance, He had spoken to me through Psalm 32: "I will instruct thee and teach thee in the way which thou shalt go: I will guide thee with mine eye." I felt I could trust Him.

I went back to Wing Fung Shi at the end of November. The village people were surprised to see me, for they all thought I had returned to the United States. I had been in contact with our Children's Refuge staff all the time. Ah Hei, my former walking companion, had come and gone between my cabin hideout and Wing Fung Shi to keep me posted. But they had all kept quiet as to my whereabouts.

Now circumstances seemed to indicate that it would be wise to go to Waitsap, a city about 70 miles to the north in the adjoining province of Kwong Si. There would probably be a bank there and also a telegraph office. One of our teachers, Mrs. Wong, had previously lived in Waitsap, so she accompanied me. We set out one cold morning early in December, along with my teenage walking companion, a village man to help carry our baggage, and a four-year-old boy who was to be adopted into the family of Mrs. Mo, one of Mrs. Wong's friends in Waitsap. The little boy rode in a basket while the rest of us walked all the way.

Late afternoon of the third day brought us to Waitsap, and we were welcomed into Mrs. Mo's home. The next morning we found that the one bank in the city was just closing its doors; no funds, no business. We interviewed the postmaster, but found that funds could not be transferred by money order. However, everyone we talked to urged us to move our children to Waitsap, saying that there would be some way to take care of them there.

Finally we visited the county magistrate, who was very interested in what we were doing. He told us by all means to move our children to his city, saying that our funds could come through government channels, if other ways failed. We told him we would have to have housing for the children and some land for them to plant vegetables. He assured us that wouldn't be difficult, and after a moment's thought offered us the use of the county farm.

Before I had left Wing Fung Shi, it had been suggested at a staff meeting that if we found a suitable place in Waitsap it would be a good idea to move at least the older children there. Since the advance of the Japanese through that quiet mountain district, however, everything had been changed. Conditions were not what they had been. At the time I replied that I wouldn't look for a place, but if the Lord should want us to make the move, I would expect Him to let the invitation come from the Waitsap people. Now here was the invitation. Again we couldn't doubt that God's hand was in it.

I found a place to live in the room at the rear of the little church in the city and settled down to do my own housekeeping while I waited for a reply to the telegraph which I had sent to the representatives of China's Children Fund in Chungking, telling them where I was and how to send funds. The others returned to Wing Fung Shi to make plans for the children's long trek through the mountains.

Suddenly a rumor spread that the Japanese were coming again. Mrs. Mo asked if I would want to evacuate in case of such an invasion. When I assured her that I would, she asked if I would be willing to go ahead and stay with her children and her belongings at a place where she had friends outside the city and then at the last minute, if the Japanese did come, she could join us and we could go farther away. She was a midwife and wanted to be at her place of business as long as possible. I was glad to do that. A servant was with us to do the cooking and laundry. I more or less supervised the children's play and activities. A month passed by and the Japanese threat did not materialize so we went back to the city; my living expenses had been very graciously taken care of.

182

CHAPTER TWENTY-FIVE

We Wait in Waitsap

* * *

I met the magistrate of Waitsap one day on the street just outside the Yamen (the government building where the officials lived and worked). He asked me why our children hadn't come. I told him that the funds for which I had telegraphed hadn't arrived yet. We therefore had no money for the long trip through the mountains.

"I have some relief money in my hands," he said promptly. "You can have that; but the question is how to get it to them."

I suggested that perhaps I could take it to them, but he questioned the advisability of my going back into that area which was so near to where the Japanese were. "We shall see," he said and we parted.

That night the prayer uppermost in my heart was for definite guidance on getting the funds to Wing Fung Shi for the children to move to Waitsap. When I woke in the morning it was again my first thought. For years it has been my habit to read "Daily Light"; I usually keep the book open on my dresser so that I can read it while combing my hair. That morning I turned the page and the words in bold type caught my eye at once. "The Lord hath said unto you, Ye shall henceforth return no more that way."

I was amazed. "Is this Your answer, Lord?" I asked.

"Then You send someone up from Wing Fung Shi to take the money back." And my heart was completely at rest.

That afternoon two of our boys came; one was Ah Hei and the other was Chan To, the boy from Saam Tsuen who had come to us about ten years previously and was now ready for senior high school. They were delighted to know that funds would be available for moving, but said that if they were to carry money they must return on Monday without fail. That would enable them to pass through the important markets on their market days, when there would be guards on the road to protect people from robbers. It was then late Saturday afternoon, too late to go to see the magistrate. We would see him on Sunday.

That Sunday I was scheduled to preach the sermon in the little church. Before I got through I felt a malarial chill coming on and by the time I sat down, my teeth were almost chattering. I withdrew to my living quarters, crawled into bed, and let the fever take its course. By a little before four in the afternoon, I had perspired profusely and was feeling fine again. Having washed my face and straightened my hair, I was ready for the visit to the magistrate's office and took Chan To with me.

Our visit there proved timely. Someone was talking with the magistrate when we arrived, a man of authority in the area through which our children must pass. He verified the boys' statement about the necessity of starting their return trip on Monday and what was more, he gave them a note of introduction to a village elder which would make the trip easier and safer for the children when they came. The magistrate was a little surprised that I would trust two boys with the large amount of money needed for moving the children. But I assured him that they were a part of our "family" and were absolutely trustworthy. He then called in his accountant and had him give us the money, a few tens of thousands because of inflation. The boys got an early start the next morning and had a safe trip back to Wing Fung Shi.

In due time the children came, taking six days to make the trip. The weather was cold; some of them had chilblains on their toes and when they stubbed them on the stones of the rough mountain paths, they really hurt. But when they arrived at the Waitsap county farm, they forgot the hardships of the way.

In the meantime, the Japanese moved up the North River to the east of us, thus completely cutting us off from the outside world. We were near the center of a rough circle, approximately 200 miles in diameter: the Japanese were north, south, east and west of us. But they couldn't cut us off overhead. We still had a God who is able to do marvelous things. He fed us all through those months when no funds from the outside could reach us.

For my own personal support the Lord sent people who wanted me to teach them English. A group of officials in Waitsap had studied English in the university, but now wanted conversational English. Another group of young men who worked in the government granary asked me to have a class with them during their noon hour. And a high school girl came in the early mornings for coaching. They paid me well; I had enough for my needs and was able to share with the preacher and his mother, whose support had been completely cut off. However, there was not much for extras or luxuries. I had brought with me from Wing Fung Shi a thin piece of toilet soap, a remnant from the days when we had been able to buy foreign things. I hoarded it carefully, but it got thinner and thinner. Then one night after my bath, I forgot to cover it up and one of the rats that shared my living quarters ran off with it.

The magistrate was concerned that the funds for which we had telegraphed in December did not come, so he offered to let us have government rice until our funds could come through. In all he gave us about 3,000 pounds of rice. At the end of the war when we had money in hand, I wanted to pay for it as soon as possible, for the price was rising daily because of inflation. But the magistrate kept putting me off with such words as "There's no hurry"; "Wait and see." In the end we learned that he had referred the matter to the provincial government and the answer came back, "Rice used for our own needy Chinese children; no remuneration required."

In spite of the danger of tigers at night, the children had a happy life on the farm for 11 months. They profited physically. Two of our older boys had been attending an agricultural high school near Wing Fung Shi and we put them in charge of the farming. They were able to put into practice the lessons they had learned about preparing compost for fertilizer and they produced beautiful vegetables. The lessons the children learned of how God can provide when there is nothing in sight will doubtless never be forgotten. They also had the joy of leading to the Lord a farm woman who lived in the same house with them. The testimony given to the people of Waitsap by the children's lives made a deep impression. The principal of the County Normal School became one of our friends. When he saw the wholehearted willingness with which some bit of service was done by either a staff member or one of the older children, he would shake his head, saying, "The spirit of it all! I cannot understand it." We told him that it was the spirit of our Lord Jesus Christ who "came not to be ministered to, but to minister, and to give his life a ransom for many."

For 13 months during that time I had no letter from home. And of course the reverse was true also: home had no word from me. The postmaster informed me that they had instructions to accept no letters for foreign countries, so why write? Mother was nearly 80 years old and not well;

she had worked hard and was just worn out. It was natural that she should worry about her youngest daughter so many thousands of miles away in a war-torn land. But one day it seemed as though the Lord said to her, "Why are you worrying? Can't you trust Ruth to Me?" "Of course I can!" was her ready reply. And her worry was gone.

During the first part of August 1945, there was a great deal of expectancy on our part. We got little news of the situation in the outside world, but many things made us feel that at last the end of the war was near. The evening English class had just been dismissed on the night of August 10th when firecrackers began popping and banging down at the end of the street. We thought little of it; probably someone was having a wedding. But in another moment firecrackers were heard farther away, then nearer and all around us. Surely the whole town wasn't having a wedding! Could it be? What if it should be . . . the end of the war?

The preacher went out on the streets to learn what it was all about. The Christian woman who shared my rooms and I looked at each other in wonder, hardly daring to speak what we thought and hoped. Within a few minutes the preacher returned.

"The Japanese are surrendering!" he shouted as he entered the front door. "The news came by telephone from Patpo; it was received there by radio from Chungking. The chief of police is sending men to knock on every door and announce the good news."

"Praise be to God!" the Chinese woman and I exclaimed in unison.

We sat down facing each other, not knowing what to say or think—other than to thank God that the end had come. For eight years all our thoughts, plans, and work had been shaped to meet the great exigency, war. Now that it was over, we must change our thinking. We must start anew. The Lord had so definitely guided in the past, all through those difficult years, and surely He could be trusted to guide and direct us now for the work of reconstruction.

CHAPTER TWENTY-SIX

We're Millionaires!

* * *

About the first of September 1945, I returned to Wing Fung Shi and to Shiu Hing. What a difference in atmosphere there! Instead of the brooding quiet between air raids, there was a sense of peace and security. I was able to collect the bank remittance which had been received for me at the time the Japanese were advancing a year before (but how drastically it had shrunk in value). Around the first of October I returned to Koon Shan. What a homecoming it was and what a welcome I received after four years' absence. Even the dog remembered me. Writing to one of my nieces about it, I said:

> After four and a half years in evacuation quarters, I had almost forgotten that conveniences or comforts were possible. Ten days ago I went back to Koon Shan for a brief visit and when I went into the house, I could hardly keep the tears from coming. The sight of the clock, pictures on the walls, comfortable chairs, tablecloth on the table, books on the shelves, soap and tooth powder in the bathroom were just too much for me. I had forgotten I had such a home this side of Heaven. How much we have to be thankful for: our little home in Koon Shan and the church there have been kept safe for us when almost all the rest of the town is in ruins.

> More than 20 years previously God had planned ahead

189

for this crisis by sending those two German sisters to work with us in Koon Shan. The work in Sai Ch'iu was precious to Him and He had known that the time would come when because of the war I would have to leave. He had provided His servants of an acceptable nationality who could carry on during those years.

While in Koon Shan at that time, I learned that Mr. Raetz, originally a missionary with the South China Boat Mission, had come to Canton and that he had money for us. During the latter part of the war, he became the representative for China's Children Fund. He was in Kunming and by applying for a chaplain's position with the U.S.armed forces, he was allowed to stay on when all other "nonessential" Americans were evacuated. Our funds from my supporters at home and from the CCF had come to him and because he was in the military, he could hold them in U.S. currency for us. The money for which I had telegraphed in December 1944 had arrived. Reckoning in Chinese currency, we were millionaires! I wrote home to Mother:

There had been a time in Waitsap when I began to wonder whether the folks at home still cared or not and I had prayed that you would all be reminded to pray even though you had no letters from me. And now Mr. Raetz has given me this long, long list of generous gifts which means that you folks not only remembered and cared and prayed, but that you were regularly sending a substantial proof of the fact that you did care. I felt ashamed that I had ever dared to doubt and I was overwhelmed with this further token of God's love and providence. The total of the amount in Mr. Raetz's keeping for us comes to over $6,000 US, which, I am told, means over six million in Chinese national currency! Now we must ask the Lord to give us great wisdom as to how to use such a husky young fortune.

I took the two German sisters with me to Shiu Hing, Luk

Po, and Wing Fung Shi. How they enjoyed the mountain scenery and seeing the younger children (it seemed quiet with all the older ones away at Waitsap). From there we went on to Waitsap and were robbed at the border between Kwong Tung and Kwong Si provinces.

The robbers relieved us of what little baggage we were carrying, which included Sister Marie Luise's passport and my glasses. But they didn't search our persons so didn't get the few thousand national currency dollars that I had in an inside pocket. The authorities in Waitsap were sincere in expressing their regret that we had met with robbers and when it came time for our return trip they sent guards with us to see us safely across the border into Kwong Tung Province.

It was time to move the children out of the Wing Fung Shi Mountains to some more accessible place. The friends in Tak Hing City on the West River invited us to come there. They said that they had long wanted to have an orphanage, but somehow it had never materialized. Now we had the children and they had the buildings; why not get together on it? It seemed the best thing to do, at least temporarily. We packed up the children, clothing, bedding, the big rice kettles, and kitchen utensils and loaded them together with the children and their nurses on one of the shallow-water boats that plied that mountain river. It took nearly three days to reach the point where it met the West River and from there we were taken in tow by a bigger riverboat upstream to Tak Hing City.

But we weren't forgetting the needs of the people of the mountain villages. We left our evangelist, Mr. Cheung, and his family, together with a Bible woman, to carry on the work. We had done some repair work on three of the buildings we occupied there and the owners said that what we had paid out would be considered as rent paid in advance. So we would have the use of those buildings for the next ten years, it seemed. The door for the mountain people was wide open.

The first week in December, I was in Koon Shan for the yearly meeting. Representatives came from the outstations. Although in seven of these outstations there was no longer a preaching hall or place of worship, little groups of Christians had held on determinedly. Now the war was over, and they were still alive. We had the joy of seeing each other's faces once more and of telling the wonderful things that God had done for us. The station of Shek Waan reported 18 new converts baptized since last I had been with them, the majority of them of the Poon clan. Koon Shan reported three baptisms and Tai Hing Shi, one. Although Loh Hong and Sha Tau had both lost their meeting places during the war, they reported three.

Many plans were discussed at that yearly meeting: plans to repair or restore damaged or lost buildings, plans to strengthen and encourage the little groups of Christians that had been without a pastor's care, plans to reorganize an evangelistic band for village work and carry on regular evangelistic work at Wing Fung Shi. Should we reopen our Bible school, day school, start an industrial project and kindred activities? With so much of Sai Ch'iu in ruins and with the economic situation so unstable, the time hardly seemed ripe for these things. Stress was laid on the work of primary importance: evangelism. One problem confronted the yearly meeting, the great need for more consecrated men and women with training or experience for full-time Christian service. It was a challenge to prayer and dedication.

For Christmas I was back in Tak Hing City with the smaller children. It was a happy time with plenty to eat and a little gift for each one. Then Ah Hei and I took to the road again. This time we wanted to try a different route to Waitsap, to see if it would be a suitable way to move the older children from there. We left Tak Hing by the midnight riverboat going upstream. The next noon we were put ashore at the mouth of a shallow branch river. We inquired about boats going up this river, but were told that they ran only on market days and that anyway, walking upstream was quicker than traveling by boat.

We set out on the trail indicated and just at dark arrived at the little market village where we had been told there would be an inn where we could spend the night. We went first to the office of the village elder to establish our identity and to let him know the reason for our passing through his territory. He was kind and courteous, sending his assistant to escort us to the inn and to see that we were given good accommodations. The assistant told us we must get a very early start and must walk quickly in order to get through the mountains before dark. There was danger of tigers.

We were up at the first streaks of dawn and walked 11 hours that day, getting onto the plain before darkness overtook us. Night had fallen by the time we reached Hoikin City, but in the dark streets we found a shop with a little light at the door. It was a restaurant displaying appetizing food. We went in, found places at a little table, but for a moment we just stood there; our limbs had become such walking machines that it seemed they didn't know how to unbend to let us sit down. That day was my fifty-third birthday.

A Christian man in the city had seen us go into the restaurant. He and the man in charge of the little church there came to talk with us while we were eating. How good of the Lord to let that man see us, for I wanted to see them, but was too tired to go and look for them. I wanted to find out if it would be possible for our children to spend a night or two in the church if we brought them this way on our way back from Waitsap. They assured me of their cooperation. They then escorted us to what was considered the best inn in the city which was more like a hotel than what we had been accustomed to.

The next morning we were once more on our way early. There was a long way to go, but no mountains and no tigers. We stopped at one place to consult with the village elder to see if our children could find accommodation for the night if we brought them by this route on our way back from Waitsap. He was willing and showed us a place where they could stay. At the village where we spent the next night, we again inquired about accommodations for the children and had a favorable reply. Early the next afternoon we were back at Waitsap and could report that we had found a shorter route for them to return to Tak Hing.

We harvested our garden produce. A big basket of fresh vegetables was taken to the magistrate who had been so kind to us. Ducks were killed, some sold and others "pressed" or sun-dried for food on the way. Then we packed clothing and bedding in bundles convenient for carrying and set out on the first lap of our homeward journey.

Three days of walking in short stages brought us to Hoikin City. We spent about three days there in the commodious church building waiting for a shallow-water boat that would take us through the mountains down to the West River.

Our party of fifty children and ten adults occupied most of the boat; the crew had reserved space at the back for themselves and for about six businessmen who were their regular passengers. There was just enough room for us to sit cross-legged on the floor in the daytime. When it came to lying down at night, we were like the proverbial canned sardines. We put the four 18- to 19-year-old boys out on the pointed prow of the boat. The boys rigged up a blanket on a pole which protected them from the heavy dew. Back of them we hung a sheet and I with the other five women occupied that space. The girls were at our feet and the boys next. There was no room for privacy and no opportunity for changing our clothes except as one of our number held a sheet across a corner. It wasn't really surprising then when we at last arrived at Tak Hing to find ourselves alive with "seam squirrels" (lice).

Whenever the boat got stuck on a sandbar, which was quite frequently, the children got off to play on the riverbank. The river was winding and the delays were frequent. It took eight days for the boat to reach the point from which my companion and I had set out on that one day's long trek through the mountains. No wonder we had been told that walking was quicker than going by boat.

On arrival at the West River, we transferred to another similar boat and were taken in tow down to Tak Hing City. Once more our "family" was all together again and it was a time of rejoicing.

CHAPTER TWENTY-SEVEN

Home and Back

* * *

B ack in 1943 Mother's health had failed and she was no longer able to carry on in the store. My sister was taking over the management. They wished that it might be possible for me to come home. I inquired about the possibility of securing passage, but was told that nothing could be confirmed beyond India. Hundreds of people were waiting there for a ship or a plane to take them the rest of the way, eating up their passage money while they waited. There was plenty of work to be done for the Lord right where I was. He gave no assurance that it was His plan for me to leave. Now, in February 1946, just after the children had been moved from Waitsap, and it seemed that others could carry on, word came from home that Mother had pneumonia. Everything taken into consideration, it seemed best to go home.

I went to the American consulate in Canton and first apologized for not having obeyed orders in 1944 by evacuating. The man at the desk looked at me with a reassuring smile and said, "But aren't you glad you stayed?" I assured him I was.

When I inquired about the possibility of now getting passage home, he replied that he would contact the military authorities in Shanghai at once. He should have their reply within about a week, and I should be prepared to

197

leave on a few hours' notice if necessary. I had expected that so soon after the close of the war I would probably be given barrackslike accommodation on some converted troop ship. Imagine my surprise to find that I had been given a single room (not a cabin) on a ship that was making its maiden voyage. It had wall-to-wall carpeting, a bed (not a bunk), an upholstered chair, a writing desk, private bath, and full-length mirrors. Such luxury was almost unbelievable.

The ship wouldn't touch at the Pacific Coast but was to go through the Panama Canal and dock in New Orleans. I sent an airmail letter to Mother from Hawaii and received a reply by radio on the ship. She said simply, "Some better. Glad you're coming." Then a letter from her met the ship at New Orleans. She told me not to hurry home but first to visit the friends in St. Louis and Fort Worth who had given generously and prayed faithfully for the work in China. It was a rare privilege to meet and have fellowship with these dear people whom I had never seen before. But the crowning joy was to arrive back in Santa Barbara after seven years and see my own dear mother and sister and her family.

I had scarcely reached home when we received word that Sister Margarete had had a serious illness in Canton. The Hebron Mission Council at once wrote for both her and Sister Marie Luise to come to America for a much needed rest. It had been nine years since the two sisters had returned to China from Germany.

Sometimes American officialdom operates as slowly as Chinese. Months passed before the necessary permit was issued. In the meantime they were kept as busy as ever: overseeing the children's work in Tak Hing, encouraging the church work in Sai Ch'iu district, accompanying the evangelistic band on their trip to villages both in Sai Ch'iu and the mountains, acting as advisers to our young people in schools in Canton and elsewhere, and securing relief supplies from UNRRA and CNRRA for the hungry people of the country districts and for the children. At last in February of 1947 the permit was received. Then things worked quickly and before the end of March they had arrived in Santa Barbara. How my family and friends enjoyed meeting in person these two dedicated women whom they had known through correspondence since 1925.

The outstanding event of my stay at home that time was the application of one of my sister's sons and his wife, Richard and Edith Potier, for work in China. They had consecrated their lives to the Lord and wanted to serve Him wherever He chose to send them. When they knew that we had been praying for a young couple to go out and head up the work among the children and young people, they applied to Hebron Mission and were accepted. Richard had served six years in the U.S.Navy as Chief Radioman and was in the thick of activities off the coast of Japan before the close of the war. They prepared to go out for on-the-job training and were ready to leave with me when I returned in September of that year (1947).

Another happy event was our acquaintance with the Rev. and Mrs. James R. Denham. The more we saw of them and the better we came to know them, the more we were impressed that the message they had to give and the testimony of their lives was just what we needed on the field in South China. During the war so much time and attention had had to be given to material things, just to keep people alive, that now in the time of reconstruction we wanted to put the emphasis on the spiritual side of things. We felt that in Mr. and Mrs. Denham, God was showing us His choice of the ones He wanted to use in this important work. Hebron Mission sent them out in the fall for a few months' ministry (through interpreters) in all the branches of the work.

Special meetings were held in Koon Shan for the workers and Christians. They were very well attended and the Spirit of the Lord was present to bless. On the closing day five young people came forward to dedicate their lives to the service of the Lord. One was Fei Lik from the clan in a nearby village whose men had been some of the worst of the robbers to pillage and wreck Koon Shan and other villages during the lawless war years. Now Fei Lik came after an invitation from the elders of that village to come and speak to them in the evening. They offered the public square in front of the elder's office as the place of meeting.

When the crowd had assembled and the kerosene lantern had been hung at the office door, I took advantage of the opportunity to thank the elder and the leading men for the protection they had given to the mission property during the war. One of the men spoke up at once, saying, "It was your God who put it into our hearts to do that."

The Denhams had six months with us: preaching, traveling, talking, eating, and preaching again. Writing home about them I said:

I think it would be difficult to find a couple anywhere of their age (they became grandparents while with us) who could have fitted in better with conditions here than they have. They love the Chinese and the Chinese love them. They love to witness for the Lord and tell others about Jesus at every opportunity. Mr. Denham is never too tired or hurried after meetings; he willingly gives his time for personal talks with all who want to inquire more about the Lord. I think it has been especially good for Richard and Edith to have had the Denhams here with us during this time, for their mature Christian experience has enabled them to give a little word of advice or comfort here and there which has been most helpful.

It was a profitable six months in the Potiers' on-the-job

training, and in the meantime they were making progress in their language study.

It wasn't long before it became known in the village that Richard understood radios. These modern inventions for the spread of news were few and far between in our country area at that time, though a few leading men had them. If something went wrong, they brought their radio to Richard. Now Richard knew he hadn't come to China to repair radios, but rather to preach Christ—so he used this as an opportunity for the Lord. The trouble was usually simply remedied and then with two or three screws still not back in place and with screwdriver in hand, he would begin telling the man of his need for the Savior. The man was perhaps eager to be on his way, but he didn't dare to pick up his radio and leave. How did he know whether the trouble had been rectified or not and how did he know just where those two or three screws ought to go in? He was more concerned with the radio than with his soul, but by the time he left with his functioning radio, he'd had the way of Life made clear to him.

CHAPTER TWENTY-EIGHT

China Changes Hands

* * *

We decided to repair our house on Cheung Chow Island. During the war it had been stripped of its doors, windows, and partitions, leaving nothing but the four 18-inch-thick stone walls and the reinforced concrete roof. In China when having building or repair work done, it's customary to have someone on the premises to oversee the work day by day. We just didn't have anyone to whom we could delegate this responsibility. I contacted a builder whom I felt we could trust, told him what we wanted done, and then went back to Koon Shan to attend to the more important side of the Lord's work. About once in ten days or two weeks, we sent Richard down to Cheung Chow to see how the work was coming. I think that the contractor, knowing that we trusted him, did as good a job, if not better, than if we'd had somebody watch him every day.

In July 1948 we moved our 25 junior high boys and girls from Tak Hing back to Koon Shan. The course we planned for them was to be essentially practical. Bible was to be an everyday subject, in order to ground the students in the Word of God and at the same time teach them how to win others to the Savior. In addition to the usual subjects of Chinese, English, arithmetic, history, etc., they took weaving and sewing. The third-year class was to have teacher-training subjects. When these boys and girls, some already

203

18 years old, finished the three-year course they would be fitted to earn their own living either at weaving, tailoring, or teaching. We also hoped that some would want to go on to Bible school to prepare for full-time Christian service. Little did we know what the future held.

Richard, Edith, and little Nancy became more and more proficient in the language. Sister Marie Luise came back from the States well and refreshed from her stay in California, eager for another term of service. (Sister Margarete remained in Santa Barbara for a longer time and eventually went from there to Germany in 1951 and home to be with the Lord in 1956.)

I had major surgery for an abdominal tumor at one of the hospitals in Canton, Chinese doctors operating. Half of the doctors in the city were interested in the testing of the tumor and rejoiced with me that no malignancy was found.

In the fall months our Chinese evangelistic group spent most of the time going about among the villages of our Sai Ch'iu District. By actual count, they spent 52 days preaching in the villages; they visited 104 villages, preaching 152 times to an aggregate of nearly 6,000 people. They sold 1,275 gospel portions and distributed nearly 10,000 tracts. Even so, not all the villages were reached, for rain hindered the work. But the evangelists were received kindly everywhere and people were eager to hear the message even in places where a large number of the listeners were armed robbers. The door was still wide open for preaching the Gospel.

In the spring of 1949, Sister Marie Luise and I went to Tak Hing for the tenth anniversary of the opening of the Children's Refuge. I wrote home:

It was a pleasant trip from the start. That is, if you know just how to interpret the word "pleasant." In the first place, two of our Christian young people, Fei

Lik and his sister Yan Tin, took us in their canoe from here to Taai Ping, which was the first stage of the journey; we had happy fellowship together as we paddled along the smooth water of the canal between the green fields. The next day we took a riverboat. A heavy thunderstorm came up just before dark and lasted until nearly midnight, which evidently made it too wet for bandits.

We arrived at Tak Hing between three and four o'clock in the morning of the 14th. At noon there was a meeting at which several spoke on the opening of the Children's Refuge ten years ago and of the wonderful way in which God has led and cared for us all this time. In the evening we had as guests our friends of the Covenant Presbyterian Mission; it was a real Chinese feast with pork cooked in five different ways besides fish and chicken. After the usual Saturday night prayer meeting, the children put on a program of their own; they had several stunts, acting out little stories and all had a rollicking good time. Sunday was a happy day. Sister Marie Luise took one group of children in the morning and gave them an illustrated Bible lesson. Mr. Lei had come from Wuchow for the occasion and he preached the Sunday sermon; he made it so interesting that only one or two of the boys got a chance to get in a few winks of sleep in spite of late hours the previous night.

We talked over plans for the children and decided that in the event of a change of government it would be best to move some of them back to Koon Shan (those who have relatives in that area). They could thus be near to some of their own folks in case of an emergency. Our Koon Shan property could also be filled up with children rather than to let it stand partly empty to attract some who might want to use it for other purposes.

Monday evening we set out to come back downriver. We got a boat at midnight and had only just got settled when we were told to get up and climb down into the hold to avoid possible gunfire. We jumped down into a small compartment below the waterline with some 30 other passengers; we were crowded and cramped and the air was stifling. After about half an hour the "all clear" was sounded and we climbed back to our bunks. We were just about to doze off into a tantalizingly delicious sleep when we were aroused again to go below; another half hour crept slowly by and then another brief respite in our own welcome bunks. Still a third time the alarm was given; that time we had to stay below for a full hour and when we came back up it was daylight; and so the night was gone and the danger too. The "pleasant" part of the return trip was that no shots were fired.

All that spring and summer of 1949 things were happening in China and rumors were rife. Most of the northern part of the country was taken over by the Communists. They had bragged that they would be in Canton by the 19th of May; but that day came and went. After prayerfully considering the situation, we decided that since the Communists hated Americans (whom they termed "capitalistic" and "imperialistic") we wouldn't be able to accomplish much by staying on. In fact, our Chinese workers and Christians would doubtless fare better without us. It then seemed best for Richard, Edith, and Nancy to leave for Hong Kong while travel conditions were still normal. We were thankful that we had repaired the little stone house at Cheung Chow, which would assure us of a place to stay when Hong Kong was crowded to capacity with evacuees from all over China. I would stay on for a while longer and Sister Marie Luise, being German, felt she could still have some further ministry.

In the meantime we were as busy as ever, preaching the Gospel, teaching the children, encouraging the Christians, trying to keep pace with the rapidly depreciating currency, and at the same time seeking to make plans for the future. Word came from Wing Fung Shi of 13 baptisms in June. Twenty more persons were attending church regularly and memorizing Scripture verses, looking forward to baptism. Sister Marie Luise was out with our evangelistic band a good part of the time or visiting in the outstations and she reported excellent opportunities for preaching the Gospel and more openness on the part of the people than she had ever seen before the war. Even the little children in the orphanage were eager to know how they could be sure they were children of God, to be ready when the Lord came back.

That summer another very bad flood occurred, worse than the one in 1915 when I had first come to China. In Kwangsi Province a landslide swept thousands of people into the swiftly flowing river. In the Shiu Hing area 30 dikes broke, allowing the floodwater to almost cover countless villages with water reaching to the eaves of the houses. In the Koon Shan area many dikes broke, devastating the crops and killing hundreds of people while thousands were left homeless. The river doesn't flow as swiftly in that area and many bodies were picked up. Some were found to have gold in their pockets. The bodies of a bride and groom in bridal attire were found. It reminded us of the words "they were marrying and giving in marriage" and the "flood came and swept them away," "as in the days of Noah." We were glad our children had asked how they could be ready when the Lord came.

CHAPTER TWENTY-NINE

The Road Forks

* * *

During the first part of August 1949, I was in Canton to cash a check and buy gold bars with the Hong Kong currency. There was no use changing it into Chinese currency which was depreciating so rapidly that we didn't want to keep it even overnight. I slipped on the sidewalk and fell. As I picked myself up, I realized that my right arm was broken just above my wrist. I stepped into a pedicab and went right to the office of two Christian Chinese doctors who were good friends of ours. They x-rayed the fracture, set it, and put my arm in a cast—all within a few minutes of the time I had fallen and broken it. The Lord had allowed it; He had lessons for me to learn and I could still praise Him with "joyful lips."

Only a few days later, word was received from the American consul advising all American citizens to leave China. He said he was leaving and advised us to go too. I didn't plan to take much baggage with me; I didn't want to strip the house of its furnishings since Sister Marie Luise was staying on. One suitcase of summer clothing, one of winter clothing, my portable typewriter, and the mimeograph were all that I took.

I only went back to Koon Shan once more for final arrangements and last words. How hard it was to say good-bye to them all! That time I left Canton by plane for Hong

Kong. As the plane flew over the familiar streets of the old city, my heart went out in deep longing for the people of China and for our Christians in particular. The Lord's own words came to me, "No man is able to pluck them out of my Father's hand."

The South China Boat Mission had several new American missionaries expecting to study the language, but the advice from the consul presented a problem to the mission chairman. What should he do with all these single women? Not being familiar with the language or the customs, they weren't able to be on their own, and where in Hong Kong could he find the right place for them? When I learned of his dilemma, I said at once, "No problem at all! Let them come to my house at Cheung Chow."

Richard, Edith, and Nancy had been able to get a plane home in June, so the house in Cheung Chow was just waiting to be occupied by some of the Lord's children.

We filled the two bedrooms with as many beds as we could squeeze in. As yet there were no clothes closets or chests of drawers, so each had her own personal belongings in suitcases or small trunks under her bed. One of our older girls from the orphanage whose brother lived in Hong Kong helped with the housework, while the missionaries took turns planning the meals. Before long, two of the senior missionaries felt led to go back to Canton and bring down their Gospel boats to anchor them in two locations in Hong Kong harbor amid thousands of native houseboats.

After the Communists had actually taken over Canton, the Boat Mission Board assigned their new missionaries to other fields; the last to leave were two who went to work in Japan. The little stone house at the top of the cliff seemed strangely quiet.

My arm had been out of its cast just about two months when I contracted typhoid fever. Through the many years in China when good health was so essential God had blessed me with it, but now that I had time to be sick, the Lord had lessons to teach me. I was taken to the little government hospital on Cheung Chow Island (one of the nurses had worked with us when we first opened the Children's Refuge in Koon Shan in 1939) and this opened a new door of ministry. Some of the nurses wanted to learn more English; some of them needed to know the Lord. After I left the hospital, they came to me in their free time for English or Bible study and one who hadn't been a Christian opened her heart to receive the Savior. They also brought to my house a young man from the TB ward who was hungry for spiritual truth. It was a joy to see his response and his growth in the knowledge of the Lord.

At the Chinese New Year, when everyone has a holiday, we had a one-day get-together for former orphanage children, now young men and women, in the Hong Kong area. There were twelve of us, six boys and five girls, with "Ma" to round out the dozen. For a guest speaker we had a friend from the Covenant Presbyterian Mission of Tak Hing who was gifted at giving chalk talks to young people. As this friend had been on a trip to Japan and I had been fearful that he wouldn't get back in time for our get-together, I had prepared a flannelgraph message from Ephesians on taking the whole armor of God. After the chalk talk, when the young folks learned through the girl that lived with me that I had prepared a message, they insisted that they wanted to hear it also. Lunch was delayed, but that didn't matter; it was a holiday! In the afternoon we had outdoor games. Near sunset the young folks made preparations to leave in order to catch the last ferry going back to the city. It was then they brought out the boxes and bags that they had with them and opened them up. One after another laid something on the table in the living room: cakes, fruit, bottles of orange drink, tins of cookies, New Year goodies, and all sorts of food—gifts for the missionary who had taken them into the Children's Refuge when they were starving and had tided them over those awful war years.

When we first left China, we were optimistic, thinking it would be only a few months before we would be able to return. But as time went on and things tightened, we began to realize that our hopes were really wishful thinking. I keenly felt that I wanted to keep in touch with our young people; I had great hopes for them. If I should go home, I wanted to be able to correspond with them. I bought a Chinese typewriter with money sent to me by a personal friend. It was a bulky machine and required considerable practice to be able to use efficiently. But before I left for home I learned that to receive a letter from a foreign country, especially from America, would incriminate the recipient.

Sister Marie Luise had chosen to stay on in China when the rest of us left. When the Communists came into the area where she was, they made thorough inquiry about what she was doing and why. They were surprised to find she was in charge of nothing, but they left her alone. For some time she went about her work of visiting and encouraging the Christians. But the time came when even the Christians, who loved her dearly, asked her not to visit them any more. Her visits put them under suspicion with the authorities and caused them to be questioned. She applied for a permit to leave.

After considerable "red tape," she was allowed to go to Hong Kong about Easter of 1951. While there she learned about the island of Mauritius with its over 20,000 Chinese residents. She felt that the Lord would have her go there to work among the Chinese in that distant place. After a visit home to Germany she went to Mauritius to find that the Chinese there spoke the Hakka dialect instead of

Cantonese. Not daunted, she went to work and learned this dialect and had about 11 years of service there. In 1964 she returned to Germany, largely for health reasons, but she hadn't been there long before she learned of the Chinese in Holland. She went to Rotterdam in December of 1965 and has been working there among the Chinese in that busy port city although she is by now into her 70s.

There seemed to be no really good reason for my staying on at Cheung Chow and I was wanted at home. Mother was in her 80s and was practically confined to bed although her eyesight was good, and mentally she was alert. She loved to read. Her mornings were usually spent reading several chapters in the Bible, then some good devotional books or commentaries, followed by Christian periodicals. By afternoon she was ready for "Time" and "Newsweek" to keep up on current events. She was intensely interested in the Jews and watched with keen interest the developments in Israel. How I felt about her is probably best expressed in a letter I wrote to her on Mother's Day when she was 80 years old:

How can I tell you all that your love and prayers have meant to me? And how wonderful it was that even before I was born, you gave me to the Lord for His service! Then how can I ever thank you for that letter you wrote in the spring of 1913, suggesting that I have a trip to China instead of continuing at Stanford? It was upsetting at the time, but it was good upsetting. Had you not written, my whole life might have been different. But now my life is what it is because of your self-sacrifice, your loving devotion, your unfailing faith, your ceaseless prayers, and your untiring love. If my service in China has been used by God to accomplish anything, the reward for that service is yours, not mine, for it is you who have earned it. God has given me one of the richest blessings there is in the world—a Mother who truly knows and loves the Lord, who led me to know Him from earliest childhood, and who has backed me with earnest, believing prayer all through these years. I just want you to know that I truly and deeply appreciate you, my darling little mother.

I cared for her until the day before Christmas, 1953, when the Lord took her home to eternity with Him.

CHAPTER THIRTY

China-Bound Once More

* * *

E arly the next year, I received a letter from the Rev. W. C. Newbern of the Christian and Missionary Alliance in Hong Kong: "When will you come to help me in the Bible school?" My heart fairly leaped with joy at the prospect of having some ministry among the Chinese in that area. Our own little Hebron Mission had come to an end. The Lord had taken all the members of the mission board, with the exception of my sister, Helen, home to Himself. The sphere of our mission's activity had been completely taken over by the Communists, but a few of our church members and some of our young people were in Hong Kong. To go back there would be like being "next door to home."

But the invitation was to go to help in the Alliance Bible School. I felt I didn't have the academic qualifications. I had never attended a Bible institute in my life; I hadn't even graduated from Stanford University. All I could claim was that I knew the Lord, loved His Word, and was familiar with the Cantonese language. I wrote to Mr. Newbern, telling him the facts and my unfitness for the work. In due time a reply came: "When will you come?"

I wanted to be sure of the Lord's will, so I put out my "fleece," a test that required six months for the answer, but at the end of that period, the answer was "approval."

Then I applied to the Christian and Missionary Alliance to go out under their auspices. I knew that now it was almost impossible for a single person, not connected with some recognized organization, to get a visa for residence in Hong Kong. I made it clear that the mission need supply neither housing nor financial support. I would live in my own house on Cheung Chow Island, only a few minutes' walk from the Bible school. Our Santa Barbara store was still in business, so I had my living allowance from it. I was accepted. It didn't take long to get my passport and a steamship booking, and in April of 1955 I was out on the Pacific—China-bound once more.

On arrival I found that Miss Tse, a Christian from our outstation Tan Tso, was Academic Dean and Dean of Women in the Bible school. Two women from Koon Shan were already living in my house. One was faithful Yan Tin. The other was Phoebe, who although not in good health was a high school graduate and made an excellent Chinese secretary. It was like "home" to have them with me.

Word soon spread that I was back, and groups of people formerly from our area came to see me Sunday afternoons. I had been gone five years and the boys and girls in their later teens had become young people in their twenties; some of them were married. Only a few were attending church regularly. Most said they didn't feel at home in the big city churches. They wished we could have our own Hebron church where they could feel they really belonged. During the Chinese New Year in 1956 we had a reunion of all the Hebron members we could locate in the Hong Kong area, about 40 of us. It was a time of feasting on the rich things of the Word of God as well as on the New Year goodies. We voted to borrow some place to meet in Kowloon until we could buy or build a place of our own. A committee was appointed to take charge of this and I went on with my work in the Bible school.

In the fall of the year that I began teaching, the course of study was reconstructed, changing it from a three-year to a four-year course which would lead to the Th.B. or B.R.E. degrees. Among the students who applied to the school were a few who, because of the unsettled conditions in China proper or in the countries of Southeast Asia, hadn't been able to finish their high school course. They were too old to be accepted in any Hong Kong high school, yet they earnestly desired to prepare for the work of the Lord. To meet their need, a special two-year preparatory course was arranged for them.

This was my department. I found it enjoyable, especially as three boys from the Children's Refuge were enrolled in the classes. Two have since become pastors of Chinese churches, one in Chicago, Illinois, the other in Sydney, Australia. Still another of our boys had already graduated from the Bible school before I went there and was then serving the Lord in Vietnam.

I had the pleasure of seeing three brothers from the Poon family of Shek Waan come separately to the school as dedicated young men, finish the course, and then go out into active service for their Lord. Their grandfather had been converted in Shek Waan in the spring of 1916 when I was living there. His son, the father of these boys, was accidentally shot and killed during the war, leaving his widow with eight little children—five boys and three girls. She was a nominal Christian and was plunged into the depths of despair, but God used this experience, through the ministry of a dedicated Bible woman, to bring her into a deeper relationship with Himself. She took courage and with God's help raised her eight children to know and love the Lord. Two of the girls had Bible school training and married pastors; the third took the course in nurse's training and she also married a pastor. The two boys who did not attend Bible school are, nevertheless, committed

Christians; one is a teacher, the other an engineer.

At least a third of the students enrolled in the Alliance Bible School were Chinese from Indonesia, Vietnam, Cambodia, Thailand, and other Southeast Asia countries. It was a joy to see them preparing to go back to work for their Lord in their adopted homelands.

For nearly six years Hebron Church met for an hour on Sunday afternoons in a borrowed church. That was the only meeting during the week: no prayer meeting, no Sunday school, no young people's fellowship. But our people made a point to bring with them to the church one or another of their relatives or former acquaintances from the mainland who, like themselves, were refugees in Hong Kong. These people, uprooted from their clan and village associations, were much more open to the Gospel than they had been previously and some of them opened their hearts to the Savior.

We were looking for a place to buy or build, but with the tremendous building boom going on in Hong Kong, we had to settle for buying a floor in one of the multi-storied buildings. At last the Lord directed us to the ground floor in a building on Oriental Street, just near the Chinese YMCA. With the combined donations from all our people and their friends and some help from the store in Santa Barbara, the flat was purchased.

On its dedication in April 1962, our first pastor was ordained. He was Gentle Lee, the boy from Saam Tsuen. He had graduated from Bethel Seminary in Hong Kong, married, and had been teaching both in Bethel and in the Alliance Bible Seminary (now relocated there) as well as helping in our Sunday afternoon services in the borrowed location.

The Christian and Missionary Alliance had offered to take our little church under its wing and our Christians had voted unanimously to accept the offer. Being part of a recognized organization was a great help in meeting government requirements for the purchase of property. Now with our own place of worship, our own pastor, a place and time for Sunday school and for young people's fellowship, as well as for midweek prayer and Bible study, little Hebron felt it was time to grow. When we moved into the new location, someone made the remark, "You are such a small group. Why do you want so big a place?" "We expect to grow" was the logical answer. And within eight years we were looking for a bigger place. Membership had increased to more than 200.

On my seventieth birthday Hebron Church celebrated with a special afternoon service of praise to God for calling me to China 50 years before. At that service my "children," those who had been in the orphanage or in the Children's Refuge and were then in Hong Kong, presented me with a gold locket, inside of which were the names of the 25 donors. These names had been beautifully written with Chinese brush pen, photographed and then reduced in size to fit in the locket. When I thanked them for it, I told them I would wear it as Aaron wore the breastplate bearing the names of the children of Israel before the Lord. Although I have not always worn the locket, I have those names indelibly engraved on my heart. Every morning I bring them to the Lord in prayer.

After the service at the church, we went to a nearby restaurant where a big Chinese feast of 16 to 18 courses (for which Hong Kong is justifiably famous) had been prepared. There were six or seven tables seating 12 each. Of course all the "children" were there, the folks from the Hebron Church, and several old-time friends whom I had invited to join us. This feast was planned and paid for by Ah Hei, the young man who had been my walking companion on the mountain trails during the war years. Married, with a growing family, he was now in business in Hong

Kong. He had a machine shop with several employees.

While we were eating those delicious things that night, my thoughts kept going back to when these children first came to me, thin and weak from malnutrition. How God had provided for them all through those lean war years!

When Hebron Church became a reality in Hong Kong with its own pastor and place of worship, a board of deacons was chosen to serve with the pastor in administering church affairs. Among those chosen were an elderly Mr. Yeung and his wife. This man was the son of Ng Sham, the first woman to become a Christian in Koon Shan way back before World War I, the Bible woman with the happy face. He was a teenage boy in high school when I arrived in China. After graduating from high school he had gotten a job with the Chinese Customs. He married a girl from Tan Tso who had been weaving cloth in our industrial department. In the Customs service they had been transferred to many of the treaty ports in China, but together they had remained true to the Lord. They had built a nice home in one of the suburbs of Canton but had to leave when the Communists took over.

Another old-timer chosen to the board of deacons was a Mrs. Shum; she was the daughter of the Mr. Poon of Shek Waan and was a girl of about 12 when I first knew her. Now she was a grandmother. She and her husband had been living in a suburb of Hong Kong since the beginning of the Sino-Japanese war. She had taken an active part in the work of the local church where they lived, but now that Hebron was started in Hong Kong, she was eager to have a share in its activities.

Still another on the board was Ah Hei. He was the kind who, when there was a need, put his hand deep in his pocket to supply it.

The new location on Nanking Street was a second-floor flat at a favorable location. It was easy to invite people off the streets to come and hear the Gospel, so evening evangelistic meetings were well attended.

Finally I sensed that it was time for me to go home. The end of the school semester had come. The last of my examination papers in biblical archaeology was corrected and the grades handed in. I had nothing scheduled for the spring semester except library work, and others could do that. I was 78 years old and just plain tired. Then word came from Santa Barbara that my sister (two years older than I) had had a slight stroke and her mind was somewhat confused. I felt it was the Lord telling me to come home.

So in March 1971 I boarded a 747 jet liner and 16 hours later arrived in Los Angeles to find it was just the same time of the same day that I had left Hong Kong. I was met at the airport by one of my nieces and her family and also by some Chinese friends. My sister was in a convalescent hospital. She knew me and was glad I'd come home. At times she was better and we had seasons of good fellowship together until the Lord took her home about a year and a half later.

Hebron Church in Hong Kong has continued to grow. With the added opportunities for evangelistic work, there were many inquirers. Study classes were arranged for new believers, which have resulted in many being received into the church by baptism. An additional young people's group was formed and called the "Enoch Group." It was really a group of young adults who had finished their education and were working as doctors, nurses, or secretaries. They loved to study God's Word and were happy to share in meeting the financial needs of the church.

In the latter part of 1971 the church began trying to decide what the best way would be to celebrate their tenth anniversary in April 1972. One suggestion was to issue a magazine which would tell how God had blessed and led the church thus far. But they felt they wanted something more vital, more living, than just printed pages. Someone suggested sending out a missionary to some foreign field. That sounded good, but just how? And where? And who? They prayed about it and asked the Lord to show them.

On Christmas Sunday in the interim between the worship service and Sunday school, a registered special delivery letter was brought to the church. It was found to contain nine $100 U.S. bills! A note typed on hotel stationery stated that the donor was passing through Hong Kong and the gift was to be used for the furtherance of the Gospel. No name was given, merely a post office box number in the United States where a receipt could be sent. The pastor and one or two of the deacons who were in the office at the time the letter was received could hardly believe their eyes. They looked the bills over and over. Could they be real? Then it began to dawn on them that this was one way in which the Lord was letting them know that their plan for sending out not only one missionary, but several, to needy fields was from Him. He would supply.

Thus it was that when Hebron Church celebrated their tenth anniversary, they also installed the officers for this new phase of the work: sending out Chinese missionaries to preach the Gospel in whatever fields the Lord might indicate. In July they set aside a few days for a missionary convention, and a Chinese pastor from the Philippines was invited to come as speaker. He is the pastor of a church of 400 members who support 40 missionaries in different countries. So he was able to tell them how it could be done.

This goal has put new life into the giving of the church. The Christians are giving generously for the monthly running expenses as well as for repaying a loan from the C&MA. They have already undertaken to give $200 U.S. a month to Jonathan Kaan, once an orphan (then a pastor in Vietnam for about 20 years) now pastoring a new little group of Chinese in Canada. They also support another in Canada and a young man in Cambodia. One Hebron young man is now working in Lima, Peru, sent out by the Chinese C&MA Missionary Society before Hebron undertook this new role. There will be more.

At the summer youth conference in 1972, seventeen young people opened their hearts to receive the Lord Jesus as their Savior. Five, already Christians, dedicated their lives to prepare for the Lord's service. The pastor's son (now two inches taller than his father) was one of these five. This young man, 19-year-old Stephen Lee, is now (in 1974) translating this book into Chinese.

As I look back over the years of my life, my heart is full of praise to my wonderful Lord for what He has done. When I set out on that trip to China in 1913, little did I dream that the end of the story would be a self-supporting, self-propagating Chinese church with the vision of sending out Chinese missionaries to preach the Gospel in all the world.

Appendix

Adapted by permission from "Missions Map of China—an Illustrated History," copyright 1972, The Evangelical Foundation, 1716 Spruce St., Philadelphia, PA 19103.

166 a.d. Han Dynasty extends from Chinese Turkestan to Korea.

635 Arrival of Nestorian Christian monk Alopen. At the beginning of T'ang Dynasty, China represents highest form of civilization in world. Nestorian adherents found only among foreign elements of the population; negligible impact on Chinese.

1215 Genghis Khan welds Mongols into world power. Campaign beginning 1236 overruns Eastern Europe, prompting diplomatic missions from Pope to seek relief from future attack. Nicolo and Maffeo Polo, Venetian traders, reach Kublai Khan's court in early 1260s, return to Europe in 1269 with request from Khan for Christian missionaries to teach doctrines and Western knowledge. Missionaries are not forthcoming.

1294 Franciscan missionary, John of Monte Corvino, arrives in Peking. Translates New Testament and Psalms; 100,000 converts by 1330; but Chinese are not brought into church leadership. Monasteries and clergy remain European.

1368 Last of Mongol emperors expelled and a new Chinese dynasty, Ming ("Great Brilliance"), ushers in one of China's greatest periods of domestic peace and cultural development. Nestorian and Western Christianity lose favor due to association with foreigners.

1552 Jesuit missionary Francis Xavier leaves Japan and settles in Macao, hoping to bring Christianity to mainland, but falls ill and dies.

1583 Jesuits Ricci and Ruggerius settle near Canton and quietly set about learning the language and culture of China. Gradually gain respect of local officials who admire their scholarship. Ricci reaches Peking in 1601 and wins official favor for work of fellow missionaries; 250,000 converts by 1650.

1664 Fall of Ming Dynasty. Manchus (Manchurians) take over in Peking. First two Manchu emperors, ruling a total of 130 years, bring China to highest point in her history. Empire stretches from Tibet to Manchuria.

1717 New restrictions on foreigners. Propagation of Christian faith also prohibited. Missionaries widely ignore edict, so new government edict in 1724 calls for expulsion of all missionaries to Macao.

1807 Robert Morrison (London Missionary Society), first Protestant missionary to China, arrives in Canton. Freedom is very limited; native Chinese are prohibited from teaching language to foreigners. But with help of two Roman Catholic Chinese, Morrison masters Mandarin and is hired by East India Company as translator. Translates entire Bible by 1819. Publication of Christian literature forbidden. Constant fear of arrest.

1822 British and Foreign Bible Society publishes first Protestant Bibles in Chinese.

1829 First American missionaries sent out by American Board of Commissioners E. C. Bridgman (1829), S. Wells Williams (1833) and Dr. Peter Parker (1834). Bridgman known for his periodical "The Chinese Repository," which brings English-speaking world news of China missions, trade, political and cultural development; Williams known for his authoritative "The Middle Kingdom" (history of China); Parker, China's first medical missionary, establishes Ophthalmic Hospital in Canton. Williams and Parker eventually enter U.S. diplomatic service in China and influence subsequent treaties which affect government policy toward work of Christian missionaries.

1842 Treaty of Nanking follows "Opium War." Compels China to remove trading restrictions in Canton and open to Western interests four additional ports. Hong Kong is ceded to British crown for use as port and supply depot. In next five years nine missionary societies enter China. One by one all principal denominations in America and England join missionary effort in China.

1860 Ten more ports opened by Treaty of Tientsin (prompted by Western military action). Kowloon peninsula (opposite Hong Kong) added to British holdings. Written into Treaty are guarantees that missionaries can travel, reside and propagate their faith anywhere in China.

1866 Hudson Taylor lands at Shanghai with 24 fellow workers under his newly incorporated China Inland Mission. Determined to carry Gospel to 12 almost untouched inland provinces. In 1895, CIM reports 641 missionaries, 462 Chinese workers, 260 stations, and over 5,000 believers.

1888 Jonathan Goforth, Canadian Presbyterian Mission, begins nearly 50 years of ministry in China, Korea and Manchuria. Known as China's greatest missionary evangelist. In five-month period in 1899, 25,000 attended his meetings. Severely wounded in head by Boxers in 1900.

1890 Missionary agencies appeal for 1,000 new missionaries to arrive in five years; 1,153 respond. Taylor emphasizes "evangelization of China in this generation."

1894 Christian and Missionary Alliance opens headquarters in Anhwei.

1894-1895 China suffers humiliating defeat at hands of Japan. Hundreds of square miles in coastal areas are leased against China's will to Germany, Russia, Great Britain and France—all of which feeds growing bitterness of Chinese toward foreign powers.

1895 Ten-man staff of Church Missionary Society at station in Fukien Province is massacred. Anti-foreign outbreaks in various other areas uproot missionaries, destroy hospitals and mission properties.

1900 Boxer Rebellion; 189 missionaries and children killed; estimate 16,000 Chinese Christians killed, many after first being tortured. Many others recanted. Boxers finally subdued by foreign troops.

China Inland Mission and other Protestant societies, by refusing indemnity, quickly gain respect of the people. More is accomplished in the next ten years than in previous century. Revival and large-scale "people movements" toward Christ reported.

1907 Centenary of Protestant missions in China. Total missionary force exceeds 3,400, representing 94 societies; 166 mission hospitals, almost 400 schools of higher learning. Chinese members number about 200,000.

1911 YMCA, which began its work in China in 1885, holds evangelistic meetings in seven major cities; 2,732 enrolled in Bible classes. YMCA eventually established in more than a hundred colleges and universities. Dr. John R. Mott a popular speaker.

1911 The Nationalists (one of many anti-Manchu secret societies) overthrow the government. Dr. Sun Yat-sen, a Christian with Western education, returns from exile and is elected president. In 1913 Sun Yat-sen again flees into exile.

More than a decade of "anarchy punctuated by civil war" follows. Nation divided between rival warlords. Robber bands numbering thousands pillage countryside. Nationalists finally begin to reestablish their base of power in early '20s—with help in political and military organization supplied by Russian Communist advisers.

1914 James O. Fraser (CIM) opens work with Lisu tribes along Burma border; strong "people movements."

1925-1927 Peking issues sharp anti-missionary decrees demanding immediate transfer of leadership in all mission institutions to nationals; schools to register with government; religious instruction to be voluntary; 5,000 missionaries temporarily leave their posts.

In 1926 there are over 150 societies in China with 8,000 missionaries. Missionary force never again so great.

1926 Chiang Kai-shek, having already unified the southern provinces with the aid of the fledgling Chinese Communist party, begins campaign that brings northern provinces under Nationalist control. Breaks with Communists in 1927, but never succeeds in fully crushing them.

1930 Following lead of U.S., other nations join in restoring to China, after 88 years, the right to regulate goods coming into her ports. Many foreign concessions returned.

1931 Beginning in 1931, with takeover of Manchuria, Japan encroaches steadily on Chinese territory in northeast.

John and Isobel Kuhn join work begun by Fraser among tribal people of southwest province of Yunnan. By 1950 there are 100 churches and thousands of believers. Most cross into Burma to escape Communist massacre.

1934-1935 Communists flee Nationalist encirclement in Kiangsi and are hardened into dedicated guerrilla army.

John and Betty Stam (CIM) are kidnapped and are executed by Communists in 1934. In period from 1924 to 1935, 29 missionaries are killed, 80 kidnapped by robber or Communist bands.

1937 Pressured by growing Japanese threat and popular cries for united front, Chiang Kai-shek reinstates Communists to legal status. Japanese troops pour into Peking area, threatening Chinese sovereignty over much territory. Nanking government decides to fight. While Mao's forces prove effectiveness of guerrilla tactics against Japanese invaders (and in the process build popular support among Chinese), Chiang Kai-shek is forced to abandon Nanking and establishes new capital in the west at Chungking, Szechwan. Mass migration (perhaps 15 million) takes place to western provinces, accompanied by many missionaries.

1949-1951 Nationalists and Communists fail to work out satisfactory political solution. In 1949, as Communists sweep south, corruption and poor morale cause widespread defection from Nationalists' ranks; Chiang Kai-shek's forces compelled to flee to Taiwan. In Communist take-over at least 34,000,000 Chinese are executed for imperialist and capitalist crimes. Vicious purging of all imperialist influences makes missionaries a hindrance rather than help. Mass exit gets under way in 1951.

The "Three Self Movement," a church program monitored by the government, buys time for churches and leaders willing to cooperate. One by one, Wang Mingtao, pastor of Peking's largest church, Watchman Nee of indigenous Little Flock movement, and others who refuse are brainwashed, imprisoned, sent to labor camps or executed.

1966-69 "Cultural Revolution" aims to eliminate "four olds": old ideas, culture, customs and habits. Red Guards go on rampage, complete destruction of remaining vestiges of organized Christian worship and witness. Military governors finally are called upon to restore order.

1972 Chou En-lai, by welcoming President Nixon's mission to Peking, amazes world by reopening door to the West. The Kingdom of Jesus Christ in China may have not only survived the past 20 years but perhaps has quietly increased.

Glossary

Ah Hei: Miss Hitchcock's walking companion during the war years.

Ah Sui: Christian woman, abandoned by her husband, who became Miss Hitchcock's housekeeper; a very faithful helper for many years.

Alliance Bible School: Founded in Wuchow in 1899, it was the second school of the Christian and Missionary Alliance (after Nyack Missionary Training College in New York).

Sylvia Bancroft: Former Holiness missionary who served with Hebron Mission during the 1920s.

Banyan: Tree of mulberry family. Branches send out shoots that grow down and root in ground to form secondary trunks.

Bible woman: Chinese word means "woman preacher." Christian women often wanted to learn to read in order to read the Bible. Those with aptitude for learning and studying often then became Bible women in their home town. First attempt in the missionary history of China to have Chinese tell Chinese. Women preachers could go into homes and speak with other women, whereas men preachers couldn't. Bible women were sometimes initially supported by the mission ($3-$4 monthly), but sold Bible portions (published by various Bible Societies) for a copper apiece, the smallest coin available, and could keep money made. Tracts were given out free.

Edwin and Mrs. Burtt: Independent missionaries of Baptist background whom the Baptist Board refused to send to China for health reasons, but who then went independently. They founded a school for the blind.

Chefoo: Beautiful resort city on the coast of North China, where the McMullens had an industrial lace-making school to provide employment and Christian teaching for Chinese girls and women.

Mr. Cheung: Young man who became a Christian through

233

Mr. Burtt. He worked with Hebron Mission, then went to Alliance Bible School and became able evangelist with Hebron after graduation.

China Inland Mission (CIM): Pioneer mission in interior of China begun by Hudson Taylor in 1866.

Colporteur: Chinese word means "bookseller": masculine counterpart of Bible woman. (Other "sellers" in China were largely patent medicine men.)

Fat Shan: Old city of about 100,000 between Koon Shan and Canton where there was a Wesleyan hospital and schools (English Methodist).

Filature: Silk mills where rows of girls unreeled silk thread by hand from cocoons in steaming water.

Joseph Flacks: Hebrew Christian evangelist who became a member of the Hebron Board. A tailor in St. Louis, he was disowned by his family, went to Moody Bible Institute, and became a pastor and traveling preacher.

Aurora Fluker: Biola graduate who served one term as secretary-bookkeeper for Hebron Mission.

Horace Houlding: Non-denominational missionary from North China.

May Jackson: Independent missionary, formerly with the Salvation Army in San Francisco, who did pioneer work in South China in the early 1900s.

Junk: Ship native to Chinese waters. It has bluff lines, little or no keel, high pole masts, and a deep rudder.

Koon Shan: City of 20,000 at the foot of Sai Ch'iu mountain in the heart of the silk-raising area where Miss Jackson opened missionary work. It later became the headquarters of Hebron Mission.

Kowloon: Part of the Hong Kong colony on the Chinese mainland.

Kwong Tung: Province in southeast China where Hebron Mission first operated.

Kwai Che: Bible woman who was a frequent companion of Miss Hitchcock's.

Kwai Ling: Seemingly retarded woman whom the Lord healed. She became the "mother" in the Hebron orphanage.

Lei Hok Kei: Chinese pastor who came to Hebron from Mr. Burtt's work. Eventually he became the evangelist in Saam Tsuen.

Lei Sing Shau: Opium addict who became a Christian. A fine Bible teacher, he later became the leader among the Hebron Chinese workers.

Mrs. McMullen: Formerly with the China Inland Mission, she started the industrial lace-making school in Chefoo as a private business when the CIM wasn't interested in industrial work.

Mat-shed: Large or small structure made entirely of bamboo and palm leaves tied together with bamboo thongs (no nails).

Marie Luise von Mengersen: Deaconess from the Friedenshort Diakonesshaus in Germany. She served with Hebron Mission over 25 years and was last Hebron missionary to leave China (1951).

Ng Sham: Bible woman "with the happy face."

Outstations: Outlying villages and towns where a mission began Christian outreach. See map for locations.

Pedicab: Three-wheeled modern version of a jinrikisha. Front part like a bicycle where operator sits and pedals. Passenger rides in cushioned seat supported by two wheels behind him.

Peking: China's capital city.

Poon Sun Yat: Businessman, early convert in Shek Waan, who was zealous in winning his relatives to the Lord. Chinese name means "to believe in One."

Po Tak: First orphan to be received by Hebron Mission.

Saam Tsuen: K. S. Lee's village.

Sai Ch'iu: District where most Hebron missionary work was located. It is also the name of the mountain behind Koon Shan.

Sampan: Small rowboat. Chinese word means "three boards."

Margarete Seeck: Deaconess from Friedenshort Diakonesshaus in Germany who served with Hebron Mission for over 20 years.

Sericulture: Raising and keeping of silkworms for production of raw silk. Silk was main industry in the area around Koon Shan. Thousands of girls and women employed seven days a week from daylight to dark.

Shameen: Island about two blocks long which was foreign concession in Canton.

Shanghai: China's main seaport, at mouth of Yangtze River.

Shiu Hing: City on West River in South China, where Burtts had their headquarters (blind school, preaching hall, etc.).

South China Boat Mission: American mission working with class of people who lived on riverboats. In Hong Kong harbor they worked as stevedores, ferrymen, and scavengers. They had fewer ties to family and clan than other Chinese.

Tak Hing City: Fourth location of the Hebron Children's Refuge in Kwong Tung province.

Pauline Thiers: Moody Bible Institute graduate. Worked briefly with Hebron Mission as teacher in elementary Bible school for young men begun by Hebron Mission

Tientsin: Place where Sino-Japanese war broke out.

(Dr.) Paul and Margaret Todd: Missionary medical doctor who operated a private hospital in Canton. Wife was a nurse.

Waitsap: Third location of Hebron Children's Refuge (Kwong Si province in Free China).

GLOSSARY

Wing Fung Shi: Little market town to which the Hebron Children's Refuge first evacuated in 1941.

Wuchow: On border between Kwong Tung and Kwong Si provinces where C&MA had Bible school (founded 1899).

Yan Tin: Girl whose birth marked the conversion of her parents. Mother delivered from demon possession. Father later became preacher. Yan Tin grew up to be valued helper with Hebron Mission.

Ruth Hitchcock was called by God to serve as a missionary in China at the age of nine or ten.

Ruth Hitchcock on the front of a typical cart from the plains of North China.

Ruth Hitchcock in 1913 enroute to China. Her five-month tour confirmed God's missionary call to her.

Chinese women of various ages were able to support themselves through lace-making at the Hebron Mission industrial school, which gave them opportunity to learn to read and receive Christian teaching.

Po Tak, the orphan whose arrival as a
young child marked the beginning of
the Hebron orphanage.

Shek Waan preaching hall in the 1930s. Women are at right, men at left. Banners are Christmas decorations. Before the Chinese Revolution in 1911, a five-foot partition separated the men and women from one another's view.

Hebron orphanage children, mid-1930s.

Children in front of Hebron orphanage.
Ah Uen seated at right in front.

Left:
Hundreds of children were cared for from
1919-1949 in the Hebron Mission orphanage
and Children's Refuge.

Granite-paved paths were typical of Sai Chiu district. Hebron missionaries walked hundreds of miles on such paths.

Hebron missionaries in late 1920s. Left to right they are: Ruth Hitchcock, Margarete Seeck, Marie Luise von Mengersen, Aurora Fluker, Sylvia Bancroft.

Bible women in 1937. Ah Miu, seated, was
once demon-possessed. Fong Shing, fifth
from left, found the Lord through the
lace-making school.

Lei Sing Shau was delivered from opium
addiction to a rich Bible-teaching ministry.

Walking was Hebron missionaries' primary mode of travel, supplemented by riverboat. Here, Sister Margarete and Peggy Potier with Chinese helpers walk home from an out-station.

Ruth Hitchcock's parents,
Anna and Herbert Hitchcock,
on 50th wedding
anniversary (Ruth at right)
in Santa Barbara, California.

Koon Shan, a city of approximately 20,000.
Note the seven pawn-shop "towers." Hebron Mission,
church, and residence are to the right of the most
conspicuous tower, at the foot of the mountain.

**Bridge enroute to Wing Fung Shi.
Second boy was Miss Hitchcock's
walking companion during
World War II years.**

Typical rice fields at plowing time. Water
buffalo was the main working animal. A small
village is concealed behind bamboo hedge
in background.

十五年元書念留映撮徒信体全會教督基豐永慶德

Group of young believers in Wing Fung Shi in 1950.